POLICY STUDIES IN EMPLOYMENT AND WELFARE NUMBER 31

General Editor: Sar A. Levitan

The National Manpower Policy Task Force is a private nonprofit organization of academicians who have a special interest and expertise in the area of manpower. The Task Force is primarily concerned with furthering research on manpower problems and assessing related policy issues. It sponsors three types of publications:

1. Policy Statements in which the Task Force members are actively involved as coauthors.

2. Studies commissioned by the Task Force and reviewed by a committee prior to publication.

3. Studies prepared by members of the Task Force, but not necessarily reviewed by other members.

Publications under Nos. 2 and 3 above do not necessarily represents the views of the Task Force or its members except those whose names appear on the study.

This study was prepared under a contract to the Task Force from the Office of Research and Development, Manpower Administration, U.S. Dept. of Labor.

UNDERSTANDING PRODUCTIVITY

An Introduction to the Dynamics of Productivity Change

John W. Kendrick

The Johns Hopkins University Press, Baltimore and London

Manufactured in the United States of America

The Johns Hopkins University Press, Baltimore, Maryland 21218
The Johns Hopkins Press Ltd., London

Originally published, 1977
Second printing, 1980

Johns Hopkins paperback edition, 1977
Second printing, 1980

Library of Congress Catalog Number 77-4786
ISBN 0-8018-1996-2
ISBN 0-8018-1997-0 (pbk.)

Library of Congress Cataloging in Publication data will be found on the last printed page of this book.

Graphics by Mark Leemon

Contents

Tables

Figures

Understanding Productivity

1

The Importance of Increasing Productivity

The chief means whereby humankind can raise itself out of poverty to a condition of relative material affluence is by increasing productivity. Productivity is the relationship between outputs of goods and services and the inputs of basic resources—labor, capital goods, and natural resources. In chapter 2, we discuss productivity concepts and measures in some detail, but for the present purposes the notion of a ratio of outputs to inputs will suffice. Since resource inputs seldom grow much faster than population, obviously the main way that output per capita can be raised is by the growth of productivity.

There are other benefits that flow from increasing productivity. It results in conservation or saving in the use of scarce resources per unit of output; it helps to mitigate inflation by offsetting rising wage-rates and other input prices; and it increases the international competitiveness of domestic production. On the other hand, productivity changes contribute to the changing industrial structure of the economy, which necessitates reallocation of resources. In particular, the technological improvements that are a chief source of productivity advance may cause displacements of labor from specific occupations, firms, industries, or geographical areas. This raises important policy issues

1

as to how to obviate or mitigate the human and other costs of increasing productivity. But to keep matters in perspective, it should be noted that the costs of reallocating human and other resources are generally but a small proportion of the increments to real income and product attributable to rising productivity.

In view of its basic importance, there has been perennial interest in productivity as a means for realization of individual and social goals. However, in recent years there has been a renewed upsurge of interest in the subject. The slowdown of productivity growth in the latter 1960s, aggravated by the recession of 1970, was believed to have intensified inflationary pressures, retarded increases in real income, and reduced the international competitiveness of American goods. In July 1970, the National Commission on Productivity was established. Through its studies and publications, conferences, and a national public relations campaign, the commission (later known as the National Commission on Productivity and Work Quality, and in 1975 renamed the National Center for Productivity and Quality of Working Life) has attempted to increase the productivity-consciousness of Americans, as well as to develop policy recommendations. The center has been joined in this effort by other government agencies and by many private organizations.

Despite the increased attention being paid to productivity in recent years, there still are widespread popular misunderstandings concerning the nature and the meaning of productivity concepts and measures and the causes and consequences of productivity movements. Yet during the past generation there has been significant progress in measuring productivity and in analyzing its causal factors and economic impacts. The important thing is that the findings of the various productivity studies should be brought together in systematic form and made available to the general public. Only by increasing understanding of this dynamic force can policies be formulated and adopted to promote productivity to the extent desirable, to facilitate adjustments to its impacts, and to mitigate undesirable side effects.

Purpose and Plan of the Volume

The purpose of this volume is to summarize the current state of knowledge concerning productivity, with particular reference to the economy of the United States. It has been the aim of the author to write in a way that will be understandable to the non-specialist, although the complexities of some of the topics do not always make for easy reading. This volume, directed to the interested public in general, is especially intended for those who are studying for or working in specialties requiring knowledge of productivity—economists, manpower specialists, industrial engineers, union officials, business managers, and public administrators, to name a few. Whereas policy makers have a special interest in and obligation to understand productivity change, only a broad public understanding can ensure that appropriate policies will be adopted and made effective.

Since this volume is one of a series of manpower studies, it seems appropriate to indicate broadly at this stage the relationship of productivity to human resources. When the term *productivity* is used in a very narrow sense to denote labor efficiency, as revealed by work measures that compare actual output to engineered standards (or the time required to perform given tasks or to produce given outputs relative to a standard), the significance is clear. How do we train, manage, and motivate workers to achieve a high degree of efficiency in their work? This is essentially a management, human relations, and industrial engineering problem.

When productivity is defined broadly, as elaborated in chapter 2, as a relation of output to *all* resource inputs, human and non-human, the relationship of productivity to manpower seems more tenuous; but it is far more pervasive and profound. In the first place, human costs and decisions are involved in creating nonhuman resources—in the discovery and development of natural resources and in the saving, investment, and production process required for the creation of tangible capital goods. Second, human skills are needed to manage and use efficiently the nonhuman, as well as the human, resources as inputs in the production process.

But the greatest challenge to the human factor is how to economize on using all resource inputs per unit of output; that is, raising total tangible factor productivity. This involves innovations in the ways and means of production: creating, adopting or adapting, and applying new technologies, organizational forms and work methods, processes, and techniques in order to obtain greater results for the same real costs. This involves human beings at their most creative, imaginative, and ingenious level. Although we generally think of innovation as being a distinctively management, entrepreneurial function, it involves the work force at all levels. The best managers build organizations that elicit creative ideas from workers generally and involve them in the innovative and adaptive activities connected with technological progress.

The results of inventive and innovative activities—in terms of growth of real incomes and changes in the structure of production—have obviously had enormous human impacts. The increasing planes of living and quality and variety of goods and services, alongside increasing leisure time made possible by productivity advance, have changed lifestyles and values. The relative growth (or decline) of various industries and occupations and the emergence of new ones have drastically altered the composition of the labor force and created problems of displacement and mobility. Rising production and population, made possible by increasing productivity, have had impacts on the natural and social environments that have created vast new problem areas, which humankind has only recently begun to confront. Clearly, many more people must know much more about productivity—its causes and its socioeconomic impacts—if we are to develop better policies to manage and to direct it toward human ends so that we may enjoy its benefits to the full while minimizing the disruptive effects. It is hoped that this volume will contribute toward that objective.

With respect to the organization of the volume, in chapter 2, we discuss productivity concepts, their measurement, and their meaning. This is basic to understanding the subsequent analyses of productivity trends and relationships. In chapter 3, the development of the relatively new field of productivity measurement and analysis is traced.

Chapter 4 lays out the productivity record of the U.S. private domestic economy over the past century, with particular reference to the period since World War II, including an analysis of the productivity slowdown in the past decade. The record of major sectors and industries is described in chapter 5, including interrelationships of productivity with output and employment.

Chapter 6 offers some international comparisons of productivity change.

The causes of productivity advance are discussed in chapter 7, with particular reference to the intangible investments designed to improve the quality and efficiency of tangible human and nonhuman resources. The economic impacts of productivity change are the subject of chapter 8.

The outlook for productivity advance over the next decade or so is discussed in chapter 9, which concludes that productivity will advance faster than in the past decade but that it will still fall below the long-term rate, unless there are special policies to promote growth. In chapter 10, various policy options for promoting productivity are discussed, as well as policies to ameliorate the human impacts of technological progress. Chapter 11 discusses policies to promote and accommodate productivity advance within the firm or other producing unit. It is fitting that the volume conclude with the microeconomic perspective, since individual organizations are where the action is with respect to the cost-reducing innovations that increase productivity, and it is at this level that the initial impacts of productivity change are felt.

Propositions on the Significance of Productivity Advance: A Preview of the Volume

The introductory paragraphs of this chapter contained a brief summary of some of the significant aspects of productivity change. Here we shall elaborate and supplement those points in terms of ten propositions that highlight the importance of increasing productivity. Each of the propositions relates to material developed in a chapter of this work. The propositions thus serve as a preview and selective summary of the volume.

1. Productivity advance results in conservation, or saving in the use of scarce resources per unit of output (chapter 2).

Reduction of inputs per unit of output, or "real cost reduction," is the opposite side of the productivity coin. Whatever the desired and attained growth of output, it is clearly advantageous for it to be achieved with fewer inputs per unit of output. This is so because the basic factors of production all have desirable alternate uses—leisure, in the case of labor; consumption, in the case of the saving that underlies capital formation; and conservation for future productive or recreational uses, in the case of natural resources. Relating output to *all* associated inputs reveals the *net* savings achieved per unit of output and thus the increase in productive efficiency.

Over the past half-century total land utilization, particularly in agriculture, has increased very little and has dropped in relation to production. The use of raw materials per unit of output has been halved—and reduced even further for domestic natural resources—as foreign sources have been increasingly resorted to. Labor hours per unit of output have been reduced by about 3 percent per year. Even capital per unit of output has been reduced by several tenths of a percent a year, despite substantial increases in capital per worker.

With regard to labor, part of the saving in unit requirements has been used to reduce average hours worked per year by close to one-half percent per annum, on average. Despite increased leisure, total hours have risen and, together with increases in nonhuman resources, have been used to expand real income and product.

It should be understood that the saving of resources that results from productivity advance need not result in "technological" unemployment (apart from temporary labor displacements) if aggregate demand grows in line with the increase in available resources and rising productivity. In fact, unemployment has generally averaged lower in periods of rapid productivity advance than when productivity was growing more slowly.

2. The expansion of productivity measurement and analysis in recent decades, associated with increasing recognition of its importance, has resulted in the development of a distinct field of inquiry (chapter 3).

Along with the development of the study of productivity since World War II has come the creation of productivity centers in most countries. These centers are devoted to promoting productivity growth and enhancing productivity-mindedness and understanding. One of the last countries to establish a productivity center was the United States (in 1970), spurred by the recognition of a retardation in the rate of productivity growth after 1966 and the various undesirable consequences of that retardation.

Regularly published statistics by government agencies and ad hoc studies by private research institutions continue to advance our knowledge of the dynamics of productivity change.

3. Productivity advance is the chief factor contributing to rising real incomes per capita in the United States and other economically advanced countries (chapter 4).

For more than half a century, since World War I, the inputs of the basic resources of labor, land, and capital, taken together, have increased more or less in line with population growth. Consequently, approximately *all* of the increase in real product and income per capita has been due to the growth of total factor productivity (real product per unit of total factor input). This improvement of somewhat more than 2 percent a year, on average, in both productivity and real income per capita has resulted in a doubling of planes of living about every thirty years. Thus, between 1917 and 1977, real income per capita has almost quadrupled. If the trend-rates of increase continue in the future as in the past, we can expect our children to be twice as well off as we are in material well-being and our grandchildren to be four times as well off. In addition, we have enjoyed increased leisure as average hours worked per year have been gradually reduced.

The technological progress that has led to cost-reducing innovations and productivity gains has also resulted in new and better products. Thus, in addition to an increase in the quantity of goods and services per capita, the variety—and in many cases the quality—of available products has also increased. On the other hand, advancing technology and economic growth have also been associated with deterioration in the physical and social environment and possibly in the quality of life. Yet income gains resulting from increased productive efficiency can be, and in recent years have been, directed in part toward slowing and possibly even reversing environmental pollution. This may result in slowing the rate of increase in productivity *as measured*, but if the quality of life could be taken into account, economic progress need not be slower.

4. Differential productivity changes by industry affect the industrial composition of gross national product (GNP) and employment. Through their correlation with relative changes in unit costs and prices, relative productivity changes affect relative sales and output. Given the relative changes in output, productivity changes determine the requirements for labor and other resources in the various industries of the economy (chapter 5).

Since the firms of the same and different industries all compete in the factor markets, average hourly earnings and the price of capital tend to rise at similar rates over the long run in various industries. Hence, relative changes in unit costs and prices are negatively correlated with relative changes in productivity, by industry. To the extent that demand is sensitive to price changes, relative changes in sales and output are positively correlated with relative productivity changes. Regression analysis shows that this is indeed the case for most industries. The relation is strong enough to result in as big an increase of employment in the industries with above-average productivity gains as in those with below-average gains, on average.

For reasons explained in chapter 5, there are two major exceptions to this rule: the extractive and service sectors. In extractive industries, although productivity gains have generally been high and relative prices have fallen, employment in farming and in most mineral industries has dropped. In service industries, productivity gains have been generally below average, and relative prices have risen; yet employment has risen faster in the service sector than in the economy as a whole.

Although industry productivity and employment changes are not systematically correlated, the underlying technological and other dynamic changes cause displacement of labor in various industries, occupations, and regions, creating problems of job security and labor mobility.

5. International differences in productivity trends create differences in growth of real income per capita and contribute to

changes in the relative purchasing power of currencies. Further, through their influence on relative costs and prices, productivity changes by industry are a crucial element affecting the international competitiveness of those American industries for which foreign trade is important (chapter 6).

If productivity advances are less in certain industries relative to the national average in the United States than in the economies of our major trading partners, U.S. prices for products of those industries will tend to rise in relation to prices abroad for comparable products, reducing exports, raising imports or both, other things being equal. Conversely, international competitiveness is improved for those industries whose relative productivity is rising more at home than abroad, on average.

Thus, industry shifts in employment are affected not only by relative productivity changes at home, as noted in point 4 above, but also by relative changes in comparison with industries abroad. This is the source of pressures—brought to bear by domestic industries whose comparative costs are rising—for protection from foreign competition or at least for measures to cushion the impacts of a deteriorating trade balance on domestic production and employment The fundamental attack on the problem is through improving relative productivity performance. It must be recognized, however, that not all domestic industries can do better than their foreign competitors in relation to national productivity trends.

6. Increases in productivity are not costless; they result chiefly from intangible investments—in research and development, education and training, health, safety, and mobility—designed to improve the quality and efficiency of the human and non-human factors in which they are embodied (chapter 7).

Other factors affecting productivity growth are economies of scale, changes in economic efficiency, and changes in the inherent quality of resources. In the short run, productivity is influenced by cyclical changes in rates of utilization of capacity and by changes in actual labor efficiency relative to potential under given technologies.

Social values, institutions, and the legal framework of the economy are even more fundamental determinants of productivity performance.

7. Productivity advance helps to mitigate inflation by reducing the impact of rising average hourly earnings and other input prices on unit costs and thus on product prices (chapter 8).

It is self-evident that input prices, on average, can rise in proportion to the increase in total factor productivity without raising factor costs per unit of output, since the reduction of inputs per unit of output offsets the increase of input prices. Product prices would also remain stable, assuming no change in profits and indirect business taxes per dollar of sales. With the same qualifications, one can state more generally that output prices rise by less than input prices, both in proportion to the increase in total factor productivity in the economy as a whole and in proportion to the increase in total productivity (including intermediate inputs) in individual industries.

The relationship between unit costs and prices over the business cycle is an important part of the explanation of economic fluctuations involving the slowing of productivity gains before cycle peaks and improvements before troughs.

8. It is unlikely that productivity growth in the United States during the next decade will return to the 1948–66 trend-rates— 2.3 percent a year for total factor productivity and 3.2 percent for real product per hour—without additional policy measures to promote it (chapter 9).

It is likely, however, that future productivity growth will exceed the rates experienced during the slowdown between 1966 and 1976. This will reflect the lifting of some of the depressing influences of that decade, such as the bulge in the proportion of the labor force 16 to 24 years of age and the sharp drop in the ratio of research and development expenditures to GNP.

Projections of productivity by industry reveal continued significant dispersion in rates of change, associated with continued changes in the composition of employment by industry and occupation.

9. If governmental programs to promote productivity growth are desired, the central focus should be on expansion of tangible and intangible investment through increased public funding

and through the creation of a favorable environment for private investments (chapter 10).

There are other approaches, of course, such as strengthening competition where that is workable; designing regulations to provide incentives for efficiency; and formulating a vigorous and comprehensive national policy to promote science and technology, the chief element behind productivity growth. The National Center for Productivity and Quality of Working Life should evaluate existing federal programs and proposed legislation on a continuing basis with respect to their impacts on productivity.

Efforts by the federal government to ameliorate the effects of technological displacements were consolidated in the Comprehensive Employment and Training Act of 1973. This act and related legislation should be reviewed periodically in order to try to improve the effectiveness of federal measures to facilitate labor mobility and mitigate the human impacts of technological and economic change.

10. Programs to measure and promote productivity are spreading among enterprises, government agencies, and other organizations. Measurement at the organizational level helps to increase productivity-mindedness, and special productivity improvement programs help to channel constructively the heightened awareness of the importance of productivity increase (chapter 11).

The organizational programs are another way of trying to enhance management efficiency in its distinctive function of innovation and improved performance. A promising feature of many programs is the formation of joint labor-management productivity committees to involve workers in ideas and actions to raise productive efficiency.

To a considerable extent, firms accommodate labor impacts of technological change through retraining and transfers within the firm. To an increasing extent, when layoffs are necessary, firms and other organizations provide severance pay and other assistance to supplement government efforts to help workers adjust.

2

The Concept, Measurement, and Meaning of Productivity

The first step in the study of productivity is to gain a clear understanding of the concepts behind the measures of productivity that are used for analysis of its role in the economy. Although there is a family of productivity measures, the unifying concept is that of a relationship of output to associated inputs, in real (physical volume) terms. So in addition to *total productivity* measures relating output to all inputs used in production, output may also be related separately to each major class of input. In this chapter, we shall consider the meaning both of total productivity and of the spectrum of *partial productivity* ratios; this is particularly desirable because there are various popular misconceptions regarding productivity. In fact, it may be useful to begin by explaining what productivity is *not* before going on to explain what it *is*.

Misconceptions Concerning Productivity

Some people use the term *productivity* as a synonym for *production*, whereas productivity properly denotes a relationship between output and the resource inputs used in production. Others interpret the term as always signifying the familiar output-per-manhour ratio, whereas productivity may refer to the relationship of output to any or all of the associated inputs, nonhuman as well as human. Even when the productivity measure is defined as a ratio of output to hours worked, it often is interpreted narrowly as measuring changes in labor efficiency or broadly as reflecting changes in productive efficiency in general. Neither interpretation is correct. Output per hour may rise as a result of substitution of capital or other nonlabor inputs for labor, not only as a result of increased productive efficiency; and labor efficiency as such is only one of the factors affecting output per hour.

Occasionally, *work measures* are confused with productivity measures. But work measures relate actual output to a norm, or standard. They thus measure levels and changes in efficiency under a given technology. They are not measures of productivity, which reflect changes in technology and other factors in addition to changes in labor efficiency as such.

The *total factor productivity* measures, which relate output to all associated inputs, should not be interpreted as measures of technological progress. They do reflect changes in technology as embodied in cost-reducing processes and producers' goods. But part of technological advance comes in the form of new or improved consumer goods, which affect the output and productivity measures only partially and indirectly. Further, although cost-reducing technological innovation is the chief force effecting changes in total factor productivity over the long run, there are other variables that affect it, particularly in the short run.

Finally, it must be noted that the *level* of a productivity ratio for any one period is not significant. Significance is derived from comparisons of the ratios for particular units, industries, or sectors over time (rates of change); or in comparisons between levels (and changes) of productivity between similar producing units or between the same industries and sectors in different countries. In other words, productivity measures assume significance in *comparisons*—intertemporal and interspatial.

Having tried to dispel some of the confusion about productivity concepts and their meaning, we shall now take the positive approach.

The Concept and Measurement of Productivity

Productivity is the realtionship between output of goods and services (O) and the inputs (I) of resources, human and non-human, used in the production process; the relationship is usually expressed in ratio form: O/I. Both outputs and inputs are measured in physical volumes and are thus unaffected by price changes. Yet constant prices as of one period must be used to multiply the units of different outputs (and inputs) by in order to combine them into aggregate measures. The ratios may relate to the entire national economy, to an individual industry, or to a company or other producing organization.

The volume of production depends on the volume of resources used (inputs) and the efficiency with which they are used. When the ratio of output to total input rises, it indicates an increase in productive efficiency, or productivity. Over the long run, total productivity advance chiefly reflects improvements in the technology and organization of production—the state of the arts. In short periods, it also reflects changes in the rate of utilization of fixed plant and equipment and, possibly, changes in labor efficiency.

Output may also be related to individual classes of inputs—such as labor (hours), man-made capital, and land—or to subcategories of these classes. These partial productivity ratios reflect changes in input proportions, or factor substitutions, as well as changes in productive efficiency.

In order better to understand productivity ratios as they are measured, we shall look at both output and input components and then at the several different kinds of ratios that may be computed.

Output

At the national level, the broadest measure of output is the gross national product (GNP). As those who have studied economics know, GNP is the market value of all final goods and services produced by the nation's economy—goods for consumption, private or public, or for investment to add to capacity for future production. The economy also produces intermediate products—materials and services used in further production. But the value of final products includes the costs of intermediate products; so the latter are not separately included in GNP, in order to avoid double counting.

When the GNP is adjusted for price changes through deflation, the resulting *real GNP* measures the total physical volumes of final goods and services, combined by means of constant prices as of one period. That is, apples and oranges cannot be added together except by using their prices to indicate their relative importance. But the prices of a base period are held constant through time, so that real GNP reflects changes in quantities, not in prices.

Real GNP can be broken down by industry of origin so that real product (output) can be related to factor inputs for each industry of an economy and productivity compared for different industries, as in chapter 5. Real product for an industry is measured exclusive of the purchases of intermediate products from other industries, which are processed further by the given industry. Thus, real industry product is a value-added concept— gross outputs *less* purchased materials, supplies, energy, and other intermediate products consumed in the production process. National product can be viewed both as the sum of product originating (value added) in all industries and as the value of final products. However, the gross output of each industry can be used for productivity ratios that relate output to intermediate product inputs as well as to basic factor inputs. But when intermediate products are subtracted from gross output, the resulting real product estimates should be related only to the basic factor inputs, as defined in the next section.

Resource Inputs

Labor, land, and capital, as every schoolchild knows, are the three factors of production, although it has become the fashion in recent years to reduce the number to two: human and nonhuman. These are the resources whose services, or inputs, are combined to produce GNP. For purposes of determining national income and product, the interindustry sales and purchases of intermediate products cancel one another out—so only final products are counted, as noted earlier. In other words, national product, as the sum of value added in each industry, avoids double counting.

Labor inputs are usually measured by the number of hours worked. If detailed data are available, it is desirable to measure hours worked in each major occupational and industry category and then combine the hours on the basis of the relative compensation per hour, held constant as of a particular base period. In this way the relative importance of the various kinds of work is taken into account, just as prices are used to indicate the relative importance of commodities.

Nonhuman resources comprise land and other natural resources on the one hand and the man-made tangible capital goods on the other: structures, equipment, and inventory stocks. The capital inputs may be visualized as machine-hours, for example, made comparable by the use of average hourly rental payments of a base period. For measurement purposes, however, we assume that the inputs are proportional to the real stocks of nonhuman resources, although some analysts adjust them for changes in rates of utilization.

The labor and nonlabor inputs are combined on the basis of their relative contributions to national income and product. The result is the measure of total factor input.

The Productivity Ratios and Their Meanings

. The ratio of real product to the associated total factor inputs yields the measure of total factor productivity. An increase in this ratio indicates that output has risen faster than factor inputs and thus that productive efficiency has improved. The ratios are usually presented as index numbers, which merely indicate what percentage that ratio for any given period is of a base period, which is set at 100.0. Further observations on productivity measurement are presented in chapter 11.

Of the partial productivity ratios, output per hour is the most commonly used. An increase in output per hour indicates the saving achieved in the use of labor per unit of output as a result, not only of increased productive efficiency, but possibly also of more capital goods per worker. Similarly, ratios of output to capital inputs may be computed, and these are also influenced by substitutions of capital for labor as well as by efficiency changes. In some industries output may be related to land and other natural resources. Thus, in agriculture the yield (output) per acre is computed. The ratio may increase because of the use of more labor and/or capital equipment per acre, of course, as well as because of increased efficiency of the land as such.

Only if output is related to *all* associated inputs, however, can one determine the *net* saving of resource inputs and thus the increase in overall productive efficiency. It is useful to look at the individual or partial productivity ratios as well. In some cases we do not have capital measures, so we must rely on measures of output per hour or per worker. It must be remembered that the so-called labor productivity measures tend to rise faster than the numbers of workers and of hours worked.

In the short run, productivity may be affected by changes in the rates of utilization of fixed plant or of overhead labor as output rises and falls. But in the long run, total factor productivity rises because of improvements in the technology and organization of production, including economies of scale. Technological progress is a complex matter, as we shall see in chapter 7's discussion of causal factors. It involves the basic values and institutions of a society, the volume of basic and applied research to discover new productive knowledge, engineering work to develop commercial applications in the form of new products and cost-reducing processes, decisions made by managers and owners to innovate and invest in new facilities, and expenditures for education and training by individuals, firms, and governments to enable the labor force both to create and to operate the increasingly complex technology.

Expanded Productivity Measures

Productivity ratios have sometimes been referred to as measures of the residual, since a change in productivity approximately equals the part of the change in output that is *not* explained by changes in the inputs included in the ratio. For this reason, the residual productivity measure has also been challengingly called a measure of our ignorance, since there are many elements, as noted above, that contribute to productivity increase.

In recent years there has been a growing effort to narrow the residual by quantifying many of the factors that account for productivity changes. These will be reviewed in chapter 7. But there is also a tendency to include some of the factors that enhance the productivity of labor and capital in input—either separately or as adjustments to the tangible factor inputs as estimated—without allowance for changing efficiency.

Thus, Denison has adjusted hours of labor input for the increases in efficiency due to increasing education, shortening of the length of the working year, and changes in the composition of the labor force. These adjustments caused labor and total input to rise more than in the unadjusted series, productivity to rise correspondingly less.[1] Jorgenson and Griliches have adjusted, not only labor, but also capital inputs for efficiency changes and thus have further narrowed the residual.[2]

In the last analysis, it is not very important whether qualitative variables are included with quantitative inputs or are used as part of the explanation of productivity change, so long as the variables are identified separately so that the investigator can see the components of changes in production. The present writer, however, prefers to measure inputs unadjusted for changes in quality or efficiency so that a change in the productivity ratio, or residual, brackets the entire change in productive efficiency. Then one can attempt to quantify all the variables, including increases in the qualities of labor and nonhuman inputs, that explain changes in productivity. It is this approach that is used in discussing causal factors in chapter 7.

3

The Development of Productivity Measurement, Analysis, and Promotion

Occasional estimates and analyses of productivity first appeared almost a century ago. But, as recounted in this chapter, government estimates of productivity began to be published on a regular basis only in 1940 and have since been greatly expanded in scope. The government figures, of course, have provided the basis for expansion of private studies of causes and impacts of productivity changes and differences. Productivity studies in the United States and abroad interacted with the movement in many countries, beginning about 1950, toward establishment of productivity centers. As described below, these centers have encouraged productivity analysis and dissemination of results as part of their efforts to promote more vigorous productivity advance.

The Development of Productivity Measurement

The early estimates of productivity were in terms of output per unit of labor input. Only much later were total factor productivity estimates developed; with some lag, this development paralleled the history of theoretical thought on the subject. Most of the early economists had some form of a labor theory of production and value. For example, Adam Smith wrote in 1776, "The annual produce of any nation can be increased in its value by no other means but by increasing either the number of its productive labourers, or the productive powers of those labourers who had before been employed." [1] But by the time of Alfred Marshall, in the latter nineteenth century, it had been clearly recognized that man-made capital goods, along with labor and land, constitute the basic factors of production. This laid the basis for the concepts of the production function and productivity, described in the previous chapter, which became the basis for later and more sophisticated attempts to measure total factor productivity.

The first estimates of productivity in the United States, made in terms of the output-per-hour concept, were prepared by the Bureau of Labor in the Interior Department in the mid-1880s. The impetus to the early studies was concern with the causes and consequences of industrial depression. Consideration was given to the role of technology in causing "temporary displacement of labor," although "the permanent good effects of machinery" were asserted. [2] Subsequent annual reports of the bureau contained estimates of hours and labor cost per unit of output over a broad range of products, for both machine and hand labor. Occasional articles in the *Monthly Labor Review* in the 1920s further developed labor productivity estimates for various manufacturing industries.

The Great Depression of the 1930s provided renewed impetus to the development of productivity estimates and analysis. The National Bureau of Economic Research, a private nonprofit organization founded in 1920, began a series of studies of productivity in various industries and, eventually, in the economy as a whole. [3] The earlier studies employed the labor productivity approach, but after World War II the total factor productivity approach was developed and applied in the summary studies.

Another intensive series of studies was mounted in the 1930s by the National Research Project of the Works Progress Administration. [4] Upon termination of the project in 1940, the productivity measurement work was transferred to the new Division of Productivity and Technological Developments in the

Bureau of Labor Statistics (BLS) of the U.S. Department of Labor, where it has continued on a regular basis to this day. Initially, the productivity measures covered output per hour in selected industries. Later, special plant-level productivity studies were prepared. A major step forward was taken in 1958, when annual (later quarterly) estimates of real product per hour for the entire private economy were initiated, broken down into the farm, nonfarm, manufacturing and nonmanufacturing sectors. In recent years, a set of limited international comparisons has also been published.

The sectoral productivity measures were made possible by the development of national income accounts in the U.S. Department of Commerce, which also began in the 1930s. In 1942, GNP estimates in current prices were added to the income accounts, based on a double-entry approach to national economic accounting. In 1951, estimates of GNP in constant dollars by major sector were presented, showing changes in the volume of final production in real terms (after adjustment to eliminate the influence of price changes). By 1962, the real GNP estimates were prepared for major industries as well as for sectors. It was, of course, the development of the constant-dollar estimates that made possible the BLS productivity estimates for the U.S. private economy by major sector. The Commerce Department in 1972 published estimates of total factor productivity in the nonfinancial corporate sector,[5] but unfortunately the estimates have not been continued on a regular basis. The Labor Department estimates have always been confined to the labor productivity variety, a fact that reflects the department's major concern with manpower aspects of the economy.

In contrast, the U.S. Department of Agriculture, which began publishing output-per-hour estimates in 1945, has published annually since 1961 a complete set of both partial and total productivity ratios for farming. The estimates are national in scope and cover major farming regions and selected types of agricultural production. The Department of Interior has published productivity estimates for various minerals industries.

The economic censuses conducted by the Bureau of the Census, together with its annual and quarterly industry surveys, are the chief source of the underlying data on the value and quantities of production. The price data collected by the Bureau of Labor Statistics are the main basis for the price indexes used to deflate values. The employment and hours data collected by the Bureau of the Census—and by the BLS on a more requent sample basis—are the chief source of labor input estimates.

Work continues in the private sector on productivity estimation and analysis. The National Bureau of Economic Research (NBER) publishes occasional studies, including an updating of its earlier summary study and the proceedings of a 1975 conference on productivity estimation.[6] The Conference Board, another private nonprofit institution, is updating the total factor productivity estimates originated by NBER on a quarterly as well as an annual basis. The Conference Board plans to continue publishing the estimates regularly since the government series are largely confined to labor productivity estimates.

Private investigators in other research institutions and universities continue to prepare studies of productivity, including experiments with new estimating techniques. The previous chapter took note of the work of Edward F. Denison of the Brookings Institution and Dale Jorgenson of Harvard University. Other private works are included in the bibliography. The field is so broad, ecompassing productivity developments in the United States and in other national and regional economies, by industry and by organizational units, that there is virtually no end to the knowledge to be gained by continuing research and analysis.

The Productivity Center Movement

Specialized institutional support for the measurement, analysis, and promotion of productivity was provided by the establishment of productivity centers in many nations during the years after World War II. The immense job of reconstruction in Western Europe and Japan gave the initial thrust to the movement, with Marshall Plan assistance. The succeeding challenge to achieve strong economic progress in those countries and rapid development in the less developed countries ensured continuing support of the productivity centers.

By the end of 1952 all West European nations had formed such centers. The European Productivity Agency was set up to coordinate the activities of the national centers and to exchange technical information with the United States through publications, meetings, visits of productivity teams, and other means. Financial assistance was provided by the United States until 1961. In 1962 the agency became the European Association of National Productivity Centers.

The Japanese productivity movement began in late 1953, when the United States offered Japan the same kind of technical aid it was giving Europe. The Japan Productivity Center was established in 1955. After U.S. aid ceased in 1961, the center initiated formation of the Asian Productivity Organization, which first comprised seven other Asian nations and now includes fourteen. Israel, Australia, New Zealand, and various countries in South America and Africa have also established productivity centers.

The major functions of most centers have been grouped under five broad headings: public awareness, training and development, consulting, sector studies, and research.[7] The sector studies involved not only measurement of productivity for various industries but also interfirm and plant comparisons. For some years the Organization for Economic Cooperation and Development (OECD) published *Productivity Measurement Review*. Consulting work was undertaken by most centers because management consulting firms were not nearly as common in other countries as in the United States. Training activities were also emphasized, mainly because of the paucity of good schools of business administration and technology until recent years.

The activities of the foreign productivity centers have been viewed as going through three phases.[8] In the 1950s, centers tried to incorporate productivity awareness into reconstruction and development plans, through massive public education, technology transfer, technical training, and cooperation among companies in measuring and promoting productivity. In the 1960s, there was much adaptation and expansion. Centers concentrated on improving and extending management education and keeping abreast of automation and other new technologies. Productivity was growing at a rapid rate (see chapter 7). The third phase, beginning in the 1970s, saw a growing concern for the quality of life—conservation, environmental

23

protection, and job satisfaction—and its interaction with productivity goals.

No specialized productivity agency was established in the United States until 1970; reliance continued to be placed chiefly on the competitive private enterprise system to spur cost-reducing technological advance. National conferences on productivity were convened in Washington in 1946, 1948, and 1950, but special attention to the subject waned as the immediate problems of postwar readjustment were succeeded by reasonably satisfactory rates of growth in real national product and productivity. The reports of the Council of Economic Advisers, created by the Employment Act of 1946, occasionally addressed problems of productivity and economic growth, but they placed major emphasis on stabilization policies designed to promote high levels of production and employment.

Renewed attention was focused on productivity in the late 1960s as the productivity slowdown noted earlier exacerbated the accelerating inflation, decelerating growth of real wages and eroding the value of the dollar. In June 1970 the National Commission on Productivity was created by executive order. The commission was composed of approximately thirty members, who represented various segments of the economy. It conceived of its mission as comprising three major functions: (1) educational, to sponsor studies, provide information, and promote public understanding of the significance of productivity increase; (2) advocacy within the government of policies and programs to promote productivity; and (3) providing a forum in which representatives of labor, management, governments, and other groups can exchange views on productivity.[9] In 1975 the commission was replaced by the National Center for Productivity and Quality of Working Life. Although the center receives only modest government support, it represents a breakthrough in that it is a continuing organization to promote productivity.

Relationship of Productivity Analysis to Economics and Other Disciplines

The study of productivity has grown out of the field of economics, but it involves only a portion of that discipline.

24

Economics is concerned with the efficient use of limited resources to produce goods and services according to the community's preferences and with the distribution of income and wealth—and thus with command over present and future output among the members of the community.

Productivity analysis is concerned with a basic aspect of the first function, production. As we have seen, productivity measures—by relating output to inputs—indicate levels and changes in productive efficiency of organizations, industries, or the entire economy. The increases in average productivity (abstracting from changes in rates of utilization of capacity) can be interpreted as indicating shifts in production functions, that is, improvements in the technological possibilities available to and used by producers. The productivity measures do not, however, indicate whether producers are using inputs with maximum efficiency at different levels of technology—that is, whether the input combinations at given prices of the factor inputs represent the least-cost combination. Nor do the measures indicate whether the input prices for the economy represent the marginal productivity of the factors—that is, the value added by additional units of the various factor inputs. In effect, in combining inputs for productivity measures, the market prices as of the base period are used.

Similarly, in productivity measurement we accept as given the allocation of resources among the various industries and thus the composition of output in terms of different types of goods and services. Also, the relative prices of the various products as of the base period are accepted as a basis for combining them to obtain aggregate production measures. Likewise, the existing distribution of income, which affects the composition of demand and thus of production, is taken as given.

So whereas productivity analysis treats a central aspect of economic life—productive efficiency—it does not treat the many problems of economic efficiency involved in the functioning of a system of market pricing as a means of allocating resources. Productivity analysis is not unconcerned with the efficiency of markets, however, since changes in economic or allocative efficiency may affect productivity.

In particular, the efficiency of markets—in allocating income between consumption and saving and among the various types of investment into which savings flow—is an important factor affecting the rate of increase of productivity, as will be discussed later. This is so because much investment is directed toward increasing the productive efficiency of the factors. Investment is the centerpiece of economic growth and development.

It should also be noted that productivity analysis draws on many of the tools and concepts of microeconomics and macroeconomics, as well as on the institutional and analytical content of other branches of economics, such as labor economics, public finance, and industrial organization. Needless to say, the tools of statistics and econometrics are indispensable in trying to quantify the interrelationships of productivity with other variables.

Productivity analysis has now reached the stage of development at which it is becoming a separate field of economics, or at least a subdivision of the economics of production and growth. But like so many other fields of economics, it reaches out into other disciplines as well. On one side, it borders on the natural sciences and engineering, since advances in knowledge and know-how, and their utilization in cost-reducing inventions, are a prerequisite for the innovations in the ways and means of production, which increase productivity. Although productivity trends reflect the impacts of cost-reducing innovations, to explain them for given enterprises and industries would involve identifying the underlying inventions and innovations and their rates of diffusion. There is a considerable volume of literature doing just that, as well as going into the economics of research and development (R&D), which helps to analyze the directions that applied R&D take. Further, in any attempt to project productivity trends, a major element in economic growth projections of any specificity, a knowledge of scientific and technological developments and prospects is necessary. This is particularly so if the projections are made by industry.

On the other side, productivity economics interacts with the other social sciences, particularly sociology, political science, and management sciences. Productivity levels and changes are fundamentally affected by social and economic institutions and values—especially the rewards and penalties that promote the creative, innovative, and adaptive activities associated with technological and other dynamic changes. Interacting with the institutions are the attitudes of individuals and groups toward these activities and toward the changes they bring about. For example, the attitudes of individual workers and trade union officials toward new technology affect institutional forms and practices that impact on rates of productivity advance. That technological changes themselves are a major cause of social change has long been recognized by sociologists, and the social changes react on changes in technology and productivity.

Management sciences are concerned both with psychological factors in industry and with the objective conditions for cost minimization under given technologies and for introduction of new technologies through investments and other measures designed to achieve the maximizing goals of individual enterprises. Since the rates of productivity advance in the various industries and the economy as a whole reflect the rates of productivity increase in the constituent enterprises, the productivity analyst must be concerned with management practices as well as with the broader socioeconomic environment.

So whereas the field of productivity has been built up largely by the work of economists, it stretches far beyond the confines of economics. Like many other subjects, it requires interdisciplinary study for an adequate understanding of the field. The selective bibliography at the end of this volume suggests the variety of angles from which the study of productivity has been approached.

4

National Productivity Trends in the United States

The rate of productivity change in the national economy as a whole is, in effect, a weighted average of the rates of productivity change in the component sectors and industries of the economy, examined in chapter 5. But it is useful to know the overall rate of national productivity change as a standard against which to compare the sector and industry changes. Further, national rates are closely related to changes in planes of living (real income per capita) for the population as a whole and the changes in the general price level. In other words, estimates of national productivity are useful for macroeconomic analysis, in which we deal with broad, economy-wide aggregates and averages.

Actually, the estimates discussed in this chapter relate to the U.S. private domestic economy, since there are no comprehensive estimates of production and productivity for general government or for the net foreign assets owned by U.S. residents. But the private domestic sector accounts for more than 85 percent of GNP as measured by the Department of Commerce. In chapter 5 we shall also refer to some partial productivity estimates available for the government sector.

Long-Term Trends

Reasonably reliable estimates of productivity go back to the late nineteenth century. Figure 4.1 shows the long-term upward drift of output (real GNP), inputs, and productivity ratios for the century 1869 to 1969. (Annual estimates began in 1889.) From 1889 to 1919, total factor productivity showed an average annual rate of growth of 1.3 percent, accounting for about one-third of the growth in real GNP, which averaged almost 4 percent a year [1] (see table 4.1). Beginning during World War I, the rate of productivity advance accelerated significantly. Between 1919 and 1948, despite a slower growth in real GNP reflecting the Great Depression of the early 1930s, total factor productivity grew at an average rate of 1.8 percent a year. The faster growth of productivity has been attributed to the spread of scientific management, a rapid growth of industrial research and development, the spread of mass production techniques in the 1920s, and a more rapid increase in average education of the working population. Indeed it appears that, had it not been for the Great Depression, the trend-rate of productivity would have exceeded 2 percent, which was the rate attained in the 1920s. Output per hour grew only a little faster than in the earlier period, reflecting the slowdown in the accumulation of capital per worker in the 1930s.

Since 1948 the rate of productivity advance, as shown in Table 4.1, has accelerated to 2.3 percent a year. Actually, the apparent acceleration is due to the steadier and more rapid rate of economic growth generally. There have been no major depressions in the United States since the 1930s, and real GNP after World War II resumed the growth rate of near 4 percent that had prevailed until 1929. Since population has grown at an average rate of 1.6 percent a year, real product per capita has increased by 2.4 percent a year, on average. Thus, productivity accounted for all of the increase in final production (real income) per capita and for more than half of the increase in total production.

It will be noted from table 4.1 that real product per hour grew at the rate of 3.2 percent a year from 1948 to 1969. This marked acceleration over the rate of the earlier period was due in part to

Figure 4.1. A Century of Economic Growth, U.S. Private Domestic Economy: Output, Inputs, and Productivity Ratios, 1869-1969[a]

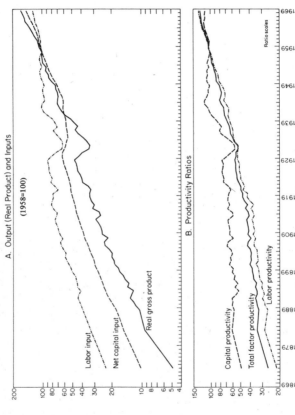

SOURCE: John W. Kendrick, *Productivity Trends in the United States*, table A–XXII; and *Postwar Productivity Trends in the United States, 1948-1969*, table A-19.

a. The pre-1889 period is based on decade averages 1869–78 and 1879–88.

steadier and stronger economic growth and in part to a rapid rate of increase of investment in capital goods per worker and per hour, amounting to almost 3 percent a year. The two factors are related, since a high rate of investment in new capital goods

Table 4.1. Productivity Ratios, U.S. Private Domestic Economy: Selected Periods and Subperiods, 1889-1973 (average annual percentage rates of change)

	Period			Subperiod					
	1889-1919	1919-48	1948-69	1948-53	1953-57	1957-60	1960-66	1966-69	1969-73
Real product	3.9	2.8	3.9	4.6	2.5	2.6	5.2	3.4	3.8
Productivity ratios									
Real product per unit of:									
Labor (hours)	2.0	2.2	3.2	4.1	2.7	2.6	3.6	1.9	2.9
Capital	0.5	1.6	0.3	0.3	-1.2	0.3	1.8	-1.0	0.2
Total factor productivity	1.3	1.8	2.3	2.8	1.9	2.3	2.9	1.1	2.1

SOURCE: John W. Kendrick, *Postwar Productivity Trends*, table 3-2, with estimates extended through 1973 by the author.

is usually associated with strong economic growth. Productivity growth from 1969 to 1973 (the latest cycle peak) was somewhat less than in the previous two decades, continuing a slowing trend already apparent in the latter 1960s, which is discussed below.

Variations in Growth Rate

So far, we have been reviewing long-run trends in production and productivity, abstracting from short-term and annual variations in rates of growth. Even the trend-rates have changed over the three periods separated by the two World Wars as we have seen. But the variations are more pronounced from year to year and even from one subperiod to another, measured from peak to peak of the expansions of the recurrent fluctuations in economic activity that we call business cycles.

The year-to-year changes in productivity (see table 4.2) are affected in part by erratic factors, such as weather. But they also have a systematic relationship to the expansions and contractions of the business cycle. Since World War II the average business cycle has lasted somewhat longer than four

Table 4.2. Output per Hour Worked by All Persons (annual percentage change) U.S. Private Domestic Business Economy, 1948-76

1948	3.9	1963	4.0
1949	1.7	1964	4.1
1950	8.0	1965	3.7
1951	2.9	1966	3.2
1952	2.5	1967	2.3
1953	3.7	1968	3.3
1954	1.8	1969	0.3
1955	4.1	1970	0.7
1956	1.4	1971	3.2
1957	3.0	1972	2.9
1958	2.7	1973	1.9
1959	3.6	1974	-3.4
1960	1.6	1975	2.1
1961	3.3	1976	4.5
1962	4.6		

SOURCE: Bureau of Labor Statistics, U.S. Department of Labor.

years, approximately one year of which has been marked by moderate declines in production. During contractions, productivity has tended to rise at less than its average rate. For example, in the recession year 1970 total factor productivity showed no increase, and in 1974 it fell. In some of the more severe contractions before World War II, such as those of 1920–21 and 1929–32, productivity actually dropped. Conversely, during expansions, productivity rose at above-average rates, particularly in the earlier stages as industry operating rates recovered and approached the most efficient rates of utilization of plant capacity. For example, although economic recovery was not very strong in 1971, output per hour rose by 3.2 percent, and in the stronger 1976 recovery it rose by 4.5 percent.

Quarterly variations are even greater than annual. Quarterly estimates show that productivity advance tends to slow down even before the peak of the cycle and to accelerate before the trough as managers seek to tighten efficiency. These tendencies are an important part of the explanation of business cycles. The slowdown before the peak tends to raise costs and to squeeze profit margins, reducing investment plans. Conversely, the pickup in productivity before the trough helps to cut costs and improve profit margins and thus contributes to the expansion of demand and production.

Even if we abstract from the business cycle as such and look at productivity changes from one peak to the next (see table 4.1), we see considerable variation. These variations in productivity advance appear to be loosely related to variations in rates of economic growth. Thus, during the strong postwar expansion between 1948 and 1953, real GNP grew at an average annual rate of 4.6 percent, and total factor productivity registered an above-average advance of close to 3 percent.

During the next two subperiods, 1953–57 and 1957–60, the rate of economic growth slowed to about 2.5 percent a year, and the pace of productivity advance also slackened. But in the next subperiod, 1960–66, the rate of economic growth doubled to exceed 5 percent per annum, and the rate of productivity advance rose to almost 3 percent on a total factor basis and to 3.6 percent on an hourly basis.

In the 1966–69 subperiod, economic growth slowed somewhat to 3.4 percent, but the average rate of advance in total factor productivity decelerated much more, to 1.1 percent a year. This was only half the rate of advance during the 1953–60 slowdown, when economic growth was weaker than in the 1966–69 sub-period. This retardation in productivity, followed by the further slump during the 1969–70 recession, led many observers to wonder if the basic productivity trend had slowed down. Even in the 1969–73 subperiod as a whole, productivity growth did not return to its 1948–69 trend-rate. It is still too early to say with any certainty that the basic long-run productivity trend has slackened. But concern over such a possibility was one of the factors that led President Richard M. Nixon to appoint the National Commission on Productivity in June 1970. Accordingly, we shall examine the productivity slowdown after 1966 in more detail. This provides a helpful background for assessing prospects for productivity growth in the future in Chapter 9.

The Productivity Slowdown after 1966 [2]

The productivity slowdown in the latter 1960s led to a number of attempts to explain the reasons for the retardation. Edward F. Denison found a retardation of 0.53 percentage point in productivity advance relative to the trend for the 1964–69 subperiod.[3] His numbers indicate that almost one-third of the slowdown was due to changes in the age-sex composition of persons engaged. The bulge in growth of the labor force in the latter 1960s increased the proportion of youth. Also, the increase in the proportion of women accelerated. Since both groups receive below-average compensation, this relative growth was a factor retarding productivity advance as measured. The rest of the productivity slowdown, according to Denison's figures, was the result of a decline in the intensity of demand relative to capacity. Denison's other forces contributed as much or more to growth between 1964 and 1969 as over the longer period since 1948 (see chapter 7 and table 7.1). In particular, advances in knowledge showed much the same rate of increase at the end of the period as throughout.

George Perry, looking at a slightly different period, 1965 to 1970, with respect to the deceleration in real product per hour (in Brookings Economic Papers, 1971) came to conclusions somewhat different from those of Denison. He found that 28 percent of the slowdown was due to the accelerated changes in the labor force mix with regard to youths and women, which is in line with the other estimates. He estimated that 36 percent of the slowdown was due to a decline in the rate of utilization of capacity, considerably less than the Denison estimate. Perry estimated that the gap between actual and potential GNP, which was 0.6 percent in 1965 and –1.7 percent in 1966, rose to 0.9 percent in 1969 and 5.8 percent in the recession year 1970.

Thus, the Perry approach indicates that other factors must have been involved in the productivity slowdown. He does not attempt to assess them, but the present writer has suggested a number of additional forces he considers important.[4] First, as is now well known, after rapid increases for several decades, research and development outlays peaked as a ratio to GNP at 3.0 percent in 1964 and declined to 2.9 percent in 1966, 2.75

percent in 1969, and 2.3 percent in 1973 and 1975. As a result, the real stock resulting from research and development investments decelerated from a 9.3 percent average annual rate between 1948 and 1966 to 6.5 percent between 1966 and 1969 and to 4.3 percent between 1969 and 1973. The deceleration of the ratio of research and development stock to the tangible capital stock was even greater, but the impact of the decline was mitigated by the fact that much of it came in the military area. Further, since the diffusion of new technology is slow, the full impact of a slower rate of increase in cost-saving new technology takes time to affect average rates of change.

The accelerating inflation that began in 1966 may well have diverted resources from productive uses and thus tended to slow productivity. More important, it eroded the real profit rate. Nevertheless, business managed to increase capital per hour (but not per worker) at rates as high as in the past, though at the expense of expanding debt relative to equity. This is all the more remarkable in view of substantial increases in national security outlays, financed in part by increased tax rates.

Finally, the negative social trends in the latter 1960s associated with the Vietnam war—increased drug abuse, crime, antiestablishment sentiment—must have had some unfavorable impact on productivity advance, although social indicators are not well enough developed to permit quantification of these tendencies and their effect. The impact would fall primarily on labor efficiency.

The factors explaining the 1966–69 slowdown also help to explain why productivity advance recovered almost back to the trend-rate during the final complete subperiod, 1969 to 1973. In the first place, there was no further sagging of output in relation to potential between 1969 and 1973. Some capacity utilization numbers suggest that the average rate of utilization was slightly higher in 1973; certainly rates were abnormally high in some of the basic industries in which investments had apparently been inadequate in the preceding years. Second, the slowdown in the increase in average quality of the labor force due to changes in mix was largely over, and the rate of increase was almost back to trend by the 1969–73 subperiod. According to the estimates of Jorgenson and Gollop the increase in labor quality, which averaged 0.7 percent a year from 1947 to 1966, slowed to less than 0.3 percent in the 1966–69 subperiod and recovered to 0.6 percent in the 1969–73 subperiod.[5] Finally, opportunities for economies of scale increased somewhat from 1969 to 1973 as the rate of economic growth rose to 3.8 percent a year, compared with 3.4 percent in the 1966–69 subperiod. The rate of increase in the real stock of know-how resulting from research and development in relation to real tangible capital (business sector) stocks, which had dropped from 6.6 percent a year in the 1948–66 period to 2.3 percent between 1966 and 1969, dropped further to 0.6 percent in the 1969–73 subperiod. But it will be noted that the rate of deceleration was significantly less from 1969 to 1973 than in the previous subperiod.

The various forms of human capital—education, training, and health and safety—continued to rise at approximately their trend-rates through 1973, according to recent estimates.[6] This contributed to the resumption of favorable shifts in the labor-force mix.

With regard to basic values and attitudes, as U.S. involvement resources, capital continued to flow toward the areas with higher rates of return. But allocations were undoubtably distorted somewhat by the wage and price controls between 1971 and 1974, which are blamed in part for the capacity shortages that developed in key industries during that period. The shortages were undoubtably aggravated by the reduced real rates of return on investment in 1973 relative to 1966, which resulted from the accelerating inflation and the restrictive macroeconomic policies invoked to deal with it.

With regard to basic values and attitudes, as U.S. involvement in Vietnam was gradually phased out between 1969 and 1973, there was a gradual healing of divisiveness and reduction in antiestablishment sentiment. Although many youths had questioned the materialistic aspects of our society, most become integrated in the workaday world just as previous generations of youth had done. Although some have questioned the goal of economic growth, the actions of most Americans indicate that they still desire higher real incomes for themselves and their children, although they are more concerned about the qualitative aspects of growth and support measures to protect the environment.

The social concerns led to legislation that had some impact on productivity—particularly the acts creating the Environmental Protection Agency (EPA) and the Occupational Safety and Health Administration (OSHA). The rapidly increasing outlays in these areas in the early 1970s, which increased costs and inputs but not outputs as measured, had a small negative impact on productivity advance. If real product could be transformed into a measure of economic welfare that reflected changes in environmental quality, it is likely that these social programs would not reduce the associated productivity measure.

In short, whereas some of the negative forces that had depressed productivity advance between 1966 and 1969 were no longer operating or were operating less strongly in the 1969–73 subperiod, the net effect of other factors was still slightly on the negative side, which prevented a complete recovery to the secular trend-rate of advance. Because of the 1973 economic contraction and the associated decline in productivity, the 1973 levels were not reattained until 1976. At the time of writing in early 1977 it is too early to tell whether productivity is returning to its old trend, but we offer some speculation on the matter in chapter 9.

5

Productivity Trends by Sector and Industry

The 2.3 percent average annual rate of growth in total factor productivity the U.S. private domestic economy has registered in recent decades is an average of different rates of change in the various industries. As we shall document in this chapter, productivity gains differ considerably in the several broad sectors of the economy and among their component industry groupings as well as among the firms or establishments that compose the various industries. These differential rates of productivity advance are associated with differences in rates of increase (or decrease) in output and employment. The technological changes underlying productivity advance are a prime source of the continual flux taking place in the economy, changes not only in the distribution of employment and other resources by sector, industry, and firm but also by region and occupational classification.

Not only are there variations in rates of productivity advance among industries, but also within industries there is greater variability in productivity movements over time than there is in the private economy as a whole. As a result, industries shift around in ranking with respect to technological progressiveness. Later in this chapter, we shall examine the causal factors that have been proved to be responsible for the different rates of productivity change in the various industries. This provides a useful background for the more general discussion in chapter 7 of causal forces and policies to promote productivity.

Productivity and Employment by Major Sector

For some purposes it is useful to break the economy down into three broad sectors, as shown in table 5.1. Agriculture is the primary sector; it consists chiefly of farming but also includes forestry, fisheries, and related activities. In early stages of economic development, primary industry is by far the largest sector however measured, but it becomes relatively less

Table 5.1. U.S. Real Gross Product Originating by Sector and Industry

	1889	1909	1929	1948	1969
	(billions of 1958 dollars)				
Total gross domestic product[a]	50.2	113.4	210.9	359.5	776.4
Sector and industry	(percentage distribution)				
Agriculture	*22.1*	*13.2*	*8.4*	*5.6*	*3.3*
Industry	*32.9*	*35.7*	*39.0*	*40.8*	*44.0*
Manufacturing	18.5	19.5	24.2	26.1	29.1
Mining	2.6	3.3	3.3	2.6	2.2
Construction	8.0	7.9	5.6	4.4	3.1
Communications and public utilities	0.2	0.7	1.8	2.6	5.2
Transportation	3.6	4.3	4.1	5.1	4.5
Services	*45.0*	*51.1*	*51.6*	*53.6*	*52.7*
Private					
Trade	15.5	15.5	17.2	16.8	16.1
Finance	18.5	25.7	{ 11.6	9.7	12.4
Services, personal and professional			{ 13.1	9.6	9.0
Governments	11.0	9.8	9.5	17.5	15.1

a. Includes imputed interest and depreciation on public capital and interest on capital of private nonprofit institutions; detail may not add to totals because of rounding.

SOURCE: Office of Business Economics, U.S. Department of Commerce; plus imputations estimated by John Kendrick.

important in the course of industrialization. The secondary sector consists of the nonagricultural commodity-producing industries of manufacturing, mining, and construction and the related transportation and utility industries. This is called the industry sector. Finally there is the tertiary or services sector, which consists of trade, finance, and other services, personal and professional, rendered both by private or public enterprises and by the agencies of general governments—federal, state, and local. The tertiary sector tends to increase in relative importance once a certain stage of industrialization has been reached.

The relative importance of the three sectors is shown in table 5.1 in terms of their shares in the real GNP (in constant 1958 dollars). There we see that, although real product of agriculture grew from about $11 billion to $26 billion over the eighty-year period, there was a steady relative decline as a percentage of real GNP from about 22 percent in 1889 to 3.3 percent in 1969. This results from two main factors. First, the demand for food increases far less than proportionately to real income per capita (since the capacity of the stomach is limited); demand for fibers has also increased less than real product, and natural fibers have been increasingly displaced by synthetics. Second, it should be noted that gross farm production has risen more than the value added—on which the industry estimates are based— because farmers have relied increasingly on industrial inputs, such as fuel and maintenance for equipment, chemical fertilizers, and commercial feed and seed.

The industry sector grew from 33 to 44 percent between 1889 and 1969, but the relative rate of growth slowed somewhat after 1929. The manufacturing and related communications and utility groups have continued to grow, while transport has leveled out and mining and construction have declined relatively. The services sector grew from 45 to about 53 percent, but since 1929 its proportion of real GNP has not changed significantly because a drop in private services, due to sharp increases in relative prices, has been counterbalanced by a rise in public services.

In order to translate these relative output movements into employment terms, we must look at the relative changes in labor productivity by sector. The numbers in table 5.2 reveal a dramatic contrast. The rate of productivity gain in agriculture (0.5 percent a year) was the lowest of the three sectors in the first period, 1889 to 1919, but accelerated progressively and was the highest of the three sectors (almost 6 percent) in the

Table 5.2. Rates of Productivity Growth, U.S. Private Domestic Economy, by Sector and Industry: Three Periods, 1889-1969
(average annual percentage rates)

	1889-1919	1919-1948	1948-1969
Private domestic economy			
Total factor productivity	1.3	2.0	2.3
Output per hour	2.0	2.4	3.2
Output per weighted hour	1.6	2.1	2.9
Output per Weighted Hour, Sectors and Industries:			
Agriculture	*0.5*	*2.0*	*5.8*
Industry	*1.5*	*2.9*	*3.0*
Manufacturing	1.1	2.9	2.7
Mining	1.9	2.9	4.2
Construction	1.0	0.4	1.0
Communications & public utilities	3.4	3.8	5.5
Transportation	2.4	4.3	3.4
Services	*1.7*	*1.6*	*1.8*
Trade	1.0	1.7	2.5
Finance		1.4	1.6
Services, personal and professional	2.2[a]	1.8	1.0

a. The 2.2 percent is for the combined finance and services group, 1889-1929; the succeeding figures are for each separately, 1929-48.

SOURCE: John W. Kendrick, *Productivity Trends in the United States*, with estimates updated through 1969 by the author.

1948–69 period. The industry sector also showed a major acceleration in productivity advance from the first to the second period but then merely maintained a rate of about 3 percent after 1948. The private services sector exhibited yet a different pattern; its rate of advance showed virtually no acceleration through the three periods, holding between 1.6 and 1.8 percent annual increase. Estimates are not available for the public sector, but there is no reason to believe that it performed better than private services. In fact, in estimating real government product, the Department of Commerce assumes no productivity advance—a practice that probably understates both productivity and real product gains.

Within each sector productivity behavior is somewhat divergent. Thus, in the industry sector, productivity in mining behaved similarly to that in agriculture, accelerating progressively across the three periods. But the behavior of construction was more like that of the services sector—it showed no acceleration. In services, the flat trend was the net effect of deceleration of productivity gains in personal and professional services offset by some acceleration in trade. We go more deeply into the industry components in the next section.

What do the sector production and productivity trends imply for employment? The picture revealed by table 5.3 is dramatic. In agriculture, the combination of slow output growth and accelerating productivity advance resulted in a major relative decline in the number of persons employed. (The table includes proprietors and unpaid family workers as well as employees.) In 1869, close to half of all persons engaged in the U.S. economy were in agriculture; a century later, only 4.3 percent were so classified. In absolute terms, agricultural employment reached a peak of about 12 million after World War I, and it has declined steadily therafter to about 3 million today.

The industry sector grew from 30 percent to 40 percent of total persons employed between 1869 and 1909. But since then productivity has grown relatively as fast as output, and the proportion of persons in industry has not changed radically, although there has been some slackening in the last twenty-five years.

In the services sector, where productivity has been growing relatively less rapidly than output, the number of persons engaged has grown steadily faster than in the total economy. The proportion was less than one-quarter in 1869 and almost 60 percent a century later. When the ratio crossed the 50 percent mark in the latter 1950s, the United States became the first service economy in the world. Although this testifies to the strength of productivity advance in the commodity-producing sectors, which permitted the shift of workers to services, it also

Table 5.3. Persons Engaged in Production,[a] U.S. Domestic Economy, 1869-1969 (percentage distribution)

	1869	1889	1909	1929	1948	1969
Agriculture	46.4	39.8	28.8	19.9	11.9	4.3
Industry	30.0	33.8	40.1	38.8	41.8	37.4
Mining	1.3	2.4	3.1	2.2	1.8	.8
Construction	4.9	4.5	5.0	5.0	5.5	5.4
Manufacturing	18.5	19.6	22.9	22.8	27.2	25.7
Transportation	5.0	6.9	8.0	6.6	5.1	3.3
Communication and public utilities	0.3	0.5	1.1	2.2	2.2	2.2
Services	23.5	26.4	31.2	41.3	46.3	58.3
Trade	8.0	9.9	11.9	16.7	18.3	18.6
Finance, insurance real estate	.4	.8	1.6	3.4	3.3	4.5
Services (private)	11.4	11.8	12.7	14.3	13.1	17.1
Households & institutions	n.a.	n.a.	n.a.	7.0	3.8	3.4
Professional, personal, business, and repair	n.a.	n.a.	n.a.	7.3	9.3	13.7
Governments	3.7	3.9	4.9	6.9	11.6	18.1
TOTAL[b]						
percent	100.0	100.0	100.0	100.0	100.0	100.0
thousands	11,332	20,660	33,535	46,216	58,795	80,092

n.a.-not available.

a. Proprietors and full-time equivalent employees. Kendrick estimates for 1929 and earlier years include unpaid family workers.

b. Detail may not add to totals because of rounding.

SOURCE: For 1929 on: U.S. Department of Commerce, Office of Business Economics, as adjusted for 1929 by Victor Fuchs, *The Service Economy*; for 1929 back: John W. Kendrick, *Productivity Trends in the United States*, table A-VII.

raises problems. That is, because productivity rises less in services, some people fear that a continued increase in the relative size of the services sector may retard productivity advance in the economy as a whole (see chapter 9).

Industry Output and Productivity Trends

Within each of the broad sectors, there is considerable diversity in rates of productivity advance in the component industries. The following discussion and productivity estimates for the various industries relate to the period since 1948, which is of greatest relevance to the current situation. Much the same pattern of dispersion in industry rates of productivity change obtained in earlier periods as well.

For the industries within each sector there tends to be a positive correlation between changes in productivity and in output, although it is not true across the three sectors. That is, industries with above-average productivity advance frequently show above-average increases in sales and output, and vice versa. The chief reason is that an above-average productivity increase means a below-average increase in costs per unit of output and, therefore, less-than-average increases in prices. Since the outputs of the various industries within each sector are somewhat competitive, customers tend to switch purchases to the outputs that are becoming relatively cheaper. So to state it more generally, industries with relative productivity increases tend to show relative price decreases, which result in relative increases in sales and output—and vice versa.

The positive association between raltive changes in productivity and in output is strong enough to counter the employment-reducing aspect of productivity advance. That is, output rises fast enough in technologically progressive industries within a sector that employment expands as much in these industries as it does in the sector as a whole.

Agriculture

The U.S. Department of Agriculture prepares estimates of production per hour worked for twelve major groups of farm enterprises, classified according to their major specialization by type of livestock and products or crop production. As shown in table 5.4, there was considerable dispersion in average annual rates of productivity advance between 1950 and 1970 in the different types of enterprises, ranging from lows of 2.3 and 2.7 percent in tobacco and fruits and nuts to highs of 8.4 and 9.1 percent in cotton and poultry, respectively. The department's estimates for earlier years indicate that there was a gradual acceleration in rates of advance during the period since 1910. As

Table 5.4. Farm Production and Output per Hour Worked, by Major Groups of Farm Enterprises (average annual percentage rates of change, 1950-70)

	Production	Output per Hour
Total	1.7	6.1
Livestock	1.7	6.1
Meat animals	1.9	3.8
Milk cows	0.4	6.5
Poultry	3.3	9.1
Crops	1.4	5.3
Feed grains	1.6	7.6
Hay	1.3	5.0
Food grains	1.8	5.5
Vegetables	0.8	3.1
Fruits and nuts	1.2	2.7
Sugar crops	2.8	5.8
Cotton	0.1	8.4
Tobacco	0.4	2.3
Oil corn	5.4	4.6

SOURCE: U. S. Department of Agriculture, *Changes in Farm Production and Efficiency* (Washington: Government Printing Office, 1971).

noted earlier, the increase in total factor productivity for the sector as a whole was considerably less than in output per hour, because of a large increase in farm machinery and other nonlabor inputs relative to hours worked. Data on the nonlabor inputs are not available by groups of enterprises, but it is fair to say that the process of mechanization and increasing capital intensity affected all of them.

Secondary Industries

For industries in the secondary or industry sector, estimates of rates of change from 1948 to 1966 in both total factor productivity and output per hour are shown in table 5.5. Note that for all industries (with one exception) output per hour rises faster than total factor productivity because of the substitution of capital goods for labor. In total manufacturing, for example, output per hour rose at an average annual rate of 2.9 percent, compared with 2.5 percent for total factor productivity. Although capital input rose faster than labor input in all industries but

Table 5.5. Industry Sector of U.S. Economy, by Groups: Output and Productivity Ratios (average annual percentage rates of change, 1948-66)

	Output	Total Factor Productivity	Output per unit of Labor Input
Manufacturing	*4.3*	*2.5*	*2.9*
Nondurable goods	*3.8*	*2.6*	*3.2*
Food (excluding beverages)	3.1	3.0	3.4
Beverages	2.7	2.2	2.9
Tobacco	1.9	1.1	2.7
Textiles	2.8	4.0	4.3
Apparel	3.1	1.9	2.2
Paper and paper products	5.0	2.5	3.0
Printing	4.1	2.7	2.7
Chemicals	8.2	4.9	6.0
Petroleum refining	4.1	3.0	5.5
Rubber products	7.2	3.9	4.0
Leather products	1.2	1.7	1.7
Durable goods	*4.7*	*2.4*	*2.8*
Lumber	2.3	3.5	3.9
Furniture	4.3	2.9	2.9
Stone, clay, and glass	3.9	2.4	3.2
Primary metal products	2.5	1.6	2.1
Fabricated metals	3.9	1.9	2.2
Machinery (excluding electric)	4.8	2.6	2.7
Electric machinery	8.0	3.7	4.1
Transportation equipment	6.7	3.2	3.2
Instruments	7.0	2.9	3.7
Miscellaneous manufactures	4.0	3.5	4.0
Mining	*2.1*	*4.2*	*4.6*
Metal	2.0	2.4	2.9
Coal	-1.3	5.2	5.8
Crude oil and natural gas	2.9	3.2	2.3
Nonmetallic mining and quarrying	4.6	2.6	3.2
Contract construction	*3.1*	*1.5*	*2.0*
Transportation	*2.3*	*3.4*	*3.7*
Railroads	0.6	5.2	5.8
Nonrail	*3.7*	*2.1*	*2.3*
Local transit	-4.8	n.a.	-1.0
Intercity passenger	0.0	n.a.	1.5
Intercity trucking	8.5	n.a	3.1
Waterways	0.2	0.5	0.7
Air transport	14.6	8.0	8.2
Pipelines	6.0	n.a.	9.1
Communications and public utilities	*7.1*	*4.0*	*5.8*
Communications	7.0	3.8	5.5
Electric, gas and sanitary services	7.1	3.9	6.1

n.a.-not available.

SOURCE: John W. Kendrick, *Postwar Productivity Trends*, tables 5-1, 5-5, and 6-1.

one, there was also some saving achieved in the use of capital per unit of output. For manufacturing and the industry sector as a whole, output per unit of capital rose by about 0.8 percent a year on average. This is important since efficiency is promoted and productive capacity expanded by economizing in the use of both human and nonhuman resources in production.

Turning now to changes in output per hour alone, we see that all industries but one (local transit) showed increases from 1948 to 1966. The increases ranged widely from highs of about 9, 8, and 7 percent a year in pipeline transportation, airlines, and electric and gas utilities, respectively, to lows of 2.0 percent in construction, 1.7 percent in leather products, and even less in intercity motorbus and water transportation.

The table also shows rates of change in output over the same period. Inspection reveals that most of the industries with high productivity advances also expanded production at relatively high rates, and vice versa. For example, local transit, which showed the only productivity drop, also showed a major decline in output as measured by the number of passengers carried. Intercity motorbusses and waterways also showed little or no increases in traffic, and this was associated with low productivity gains. Conversely, the high-productivity industries mentioned above also experienced high rates of growth of output. There were exceptions to this positive correlation, however—such as the coal industry, which was able to achieve substantial productivity gains by progressive mechanization of the mines despite a declining market for coal until recently as a result of competition from such other fuels as oil and gas.

Though not shown on the table, industries with relative productivity increases had relative price decreases. This is an important part of the explanation for the relative increases in sales and output of the high-productivity industries. Here, again, the correlation is not perfect, for sales depend on factors besides prices. For example, as noted earlier, sales of farm products grew less than GNP, despite high productivity gains and relative price declines, because of special factors, including governmental programs. Also, the positive correlation between relative changes in productivity and in output is a bit greater than can be explained by relative price behavior alone. This suggests that there is a reciprocal relationship—that high rates of production growth stimulate productivity advance by opening up possibilities for economies of scale.

Services

Less is known about productivity in the service sector—trade, finance, personal and professional and other private services, and governmental services—than is known about commodity production. But one study developed productivity estimates for eighteen selected private service industries (see table 5.6). The picture of wide dispersion in rates of productivity advance is the same as for commodities, although the average increase is lower. Thus, within the ten retail trades shown, rates of increase in output per person ranged from 3.5 percent for furniture and appliance stores and 2.8 percent for food stores (due in part to the trend toward self-service) down to 0.2 percent for eating and drinking places. Within the eight service industries studied, rates of increase ranged from 2.0 percent for auto repair and 1.7 percent each for beauty shops and dry cleaning down to negative figures for hotels and motels and motion picture theaters.

Just as in the commodity sectors, there was a significant positive correlation between rates of change in output and in productivity. For example, the big drop in productivity of movie houses was associated with a big drop in output as measured by attendance, due importantly to the competition of television entertainment at home. Again, relative price movements have a lot to do with this association. For example, productivity advance in barbering is low, so the relative price of haircuts rises, which dampens business for the barbers.

Although there is no estimate for productivity in governments as a whole, a special pilot study did develop estimates for four federal government agencies, also shown in table 5.6.[1] Here, too, there were wide differences in rates of change in output per weighted hour for varying numbers of years ending with 1962 (later estimates on an agency basis have not been published). Average annual rates of gain were only 0.1 and 0.2 percent in the Systems Maintenance Service of the Federal Aviation

Table 5.6. Productivity Trends in Selected Service Industries: Output per Person or per Hour (average annual percentage rates of change)

Industry	Rate of Change
Ten Retail Trades: Output per Person, 1948-63	
Apparel stores	1.7
Automobile dealers	2.2
Drug stores	2.3
Eating and drinking places	0.2
Food stores	2.8
Furniture and appliances	3.5
Gasoline stations	2.1
General merchandise	2.3
Lumber dealers	1.2
Other	1.1
Eight Private Services: Output per Person, 1948-63	
Auto repair	2.0
Barber shops	0.3
Beauty shops	1.7
Dry cleaning	1.7
Hotels and motels	-0.5
Laundries	0
Motion picture theatres	-3.2
Shoe repair	1.3
Four Federal Government Organizations: Output per Weighted Hour, Varying Periods ending 1962	
Department of Insurance, Veterans Administration, 1955-62	8.3
Division of Disbursement, Treasury Department, 1949-62	8.6
Post Office Department, 1953-62	0.2
Systems Maintenance Service, Federal Aviation Agency, 1958-62	0.1

SOURCES: Trade and services, Victor R. Fuchs, *The Service Economy*, table 27, p. 84; federal government, *Measuring Productivity of Federal Government Organizations*, table 1, p. 14.

Agency and in the Post Office Department (now the Postal Service), respectively. But in the Department of Insurance of the Veterans Administration the average increase was 8.3 percent a year, and in the Division of Disbursement of the Treasury Department it was 8.6 percent—as high as the increases in some of the most progressive private industries. The

49

adoption of electronic data processing equipment in these two agencies was a major cause of their big efficiency gains.

The feasibility of measuring government productivity having been demonstrated, an interagency team subsequently collected data for the fiscal years 1967–71 from 114 organizational units in 17 agencies representing about 54 percent of the civilian work force. By fiscal year 1975 coverage had been expanded to 67 percent of the work force from 279 units in 51 agencies. During the 1967–75 period output per employee-year rose at an average annual rate of 1.3 percent (see figure 5.1). This is of the same order of magnitude as the increase in the private service industry grouping.

Many of the organizational units did very well, posting average gains of better than 6 percent a year, but a significant number also registered declines in productivity. When the units are arranged by function (see table 5.7), the dispersion is reduced. Only a few functions showed declines; three functions showed average annual increases in excess of 4 percent— general support services, loans and grants, and library services. The productivity data and related investigations provide the basis for analysis of causal factors by the Joint Financial Management Improvement Program, reported below.

Remember that, although the average rate of productivity increase in the services sector was below that in the commodity sectors and although price increases (including tax rates) were higher, demand and output grew even more for services as a whole than for commodities. This is because as production and real income per capita grow, there is a relative shift of demand toward services. It is expected that the services sector will continue to grow relatively—certainly in terms of employment. This poses the challenge of trying to improve efficiency further in both public and private services.

Causes of Industry Differences in Productivity Gains

The wide differences in rates of productivity gain by industry offer a good opportunity to investigate causes for the differences. The researcher can correlate differences in possible causal factors with the different productivity rates in the various

Figure 5.1. Trend in Output per Employee-Year for Sample of Federal Government Civilian Workers, Fiscal Years 1967-76[a]

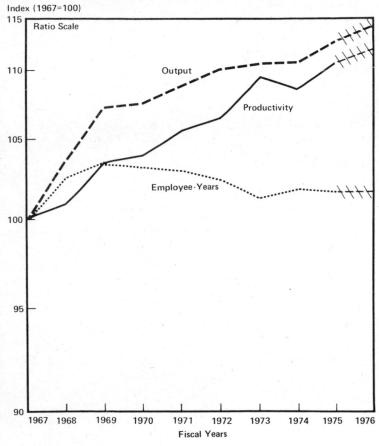

a. Data for FY1976 are preliminary.

SOURCE: Bureau of Labor Statistics, U.S. Department of Labor, *Annual Report to the President and Congress* (Washington: National Center for Productivity and Quality of Working Life), p. 51.

industries and determine which are significantly associated. The present writer, among others, has carried out this type of research for manufacturing industries and has found five factors, out of more than a dozen tested, to be significant.[2]

Table 5.7. Output per Employee-Year, Output, and Employee-Years, by Functional Grouping, Fiscal Years 1967-75 (average annual percentage rates of change)

	Output per Employee Year	Output	Employee-Years
All Functions	1.3	1.3	0.0
Product-Oriented Functions			
Specialized manufacturing	2.7	1.5	-1.1
Overhaul, repair of equipment, and vehicle maintenance	0.6	-3.9	-4.4
Facilities maintenance	0.6	-0.6	-1.3
Power	2.5	8.9	6.2
Standard printing	-2.4	-4.5	-2.1
Agriculture and natural resources	1.8	0.2	-1.6
Service-Oriented Functions			
Loans and grants	5.6	6.1	0.5
Citizen's records	2.7	6.0	3.2
Reference services	-0.1	5.3	5.5
Regulation—rulemaking and licensing	2.4	6.1	3.6
Regulation manpower and labor relations	3.2	5.9	2.7
Regulation finance	3.8	5.9	2 0
Regulation inspection and enforcement	3.2	7.2	3.9
Education and training	0.3	1.0	0.7
Medical services	-0.4	1.6	2.0
Postal service	1.1	1.1	0.0
Transportation	2.5	3.1	0.6
Support-Oriented Functions			
Procurement	1.3	-2.3	-3.6
Supply	1.4	-5.2	-6.5
Personnel management	2.1	5.9	3.7
Finance and accounting	1.5	0.3	-1.2
Internal audit	2.7	3.2	0.5
Library services	4.2	7.1	2.8
Military base service	-2.0	-5.3	-3.4
General support services	6.5	7.1	0.5

SOURCE: Bureau of Labor Statistics, U.S. Department of Labor.

First, rates of change in output are positively associated with those in productivity. As noted earlier, it is a two-way relationship. On the causal side, increases in the scale of output open up possibilities of economies through greater specialization of personnel, machines, plants, and firms. Also, some overhead functions (such as financial management) do not have to be expanded in proportion to output. Further, it is easier to innovate when adding to capacity than when replacing capacity. So relative growth of production contributes to productivity, as well as resulting from the associated relative decline in prices.

A second significant factor is the proportion of revenues spent by the firms of an industry on research and development (R&D). Most industry research is applied to the discovery of new knowledge and know-how that would be of value to the firm in developing new products or cost-reducing technology. Then comes the development and engineering work needed to translate useful inventions into commercially feasible production processes or prototypes of new products. Although productivity advances therefore obviously are related to the relative volume of funds spent for R&D in various industries, this is not the whole story. Some of the R&D expenditures made by other industries—those supplying capital goods and intermediate products to a given industry—likewise conduce to its productivity advance. Also, the R&D financed by government and universities helps particular industries. Despite this interdependence, however, the industries that spend above the average on R&D tend to have higher rates of productivity advance.

The third factor is the average education per worker. This is probably a reciprocal relationship—the technologically more progressive industries offer more skilled and professional occupations, and the workers with higher levels of education and training tend to make a larger contribution to advancing technology.

The fourth factor is the extent of cyclical variations in production. Those manufacturing industries with greater ups and downs of sales and output tend to have lower rates of productivity advance. The same can be seen outside of manufacturing; for example, the construction industry has wide swings in activity, with contractors going in and out of business depending on demand for housing and other types of buildings. This cyclical variability is associated with a below-average rate of productivity advance. In contrast, the electric utilities have had a rather steady rate of growth in demand for kilowatt-hours of power, even in recession years. This has been associated with a high trend-rate of productivity advance.

The final factor, which has shown up as negatively correlated with productivity advance, is the degree of unionization. That is, industries in which a larger-than-average proportion of workers belong to labor unions tend to have a lower rate of productivity advance than those with a lower unionization rate, other things being equal. This is perhaps not a surprising result when it is remembered that some unions restrict the amount of work members do or have work rules requiring more members of work crews than are needed. Also, unions often seek a voice in determining the pace of innovation and technological advance in firms, since they are affected by the changes. Such policies, which stem from labor's understandable fear of unemployment, are one reason why it is important for the federal government to maintain relatively full employment and to help displaced workers find new jobs.

6

International Productivity Comparisons

Anyone who has traveled much abroad must have been struck by the difference in planes of living in various countries. The traveler may also have noticed a relationship between the levels of living and the degree of sophistication in the technologies of production in use. The major element explaining these international differences in levels and in rates of change of real income per capita is the difference in levels and rate of change of productivity. Differential productivity changes also are a factor in relative exchange rates, movements of price levels, and the purchasing power of currencies. It is to the macroeconomic effects of international differences in productivity that we devote the first part of this chapter.

There also are industry differences in levels and rates of productivity change among nations, which affect patterns of international trade. These matters are discussed in the second part of this chapter. The discussion is brief, for there is a paucity of comparable statistics on productivity by industry for various countries. Nevertheless, some general conclusions can be drawn.

Macroeconomic Comparisons

From the latter nineteenth century to the mid-twentieth century, the United States had one of the highest rates of growth—measured in real product per year worked—of all advanced countries. As shown in table 6.1, only Japan has had a significantly higher rate of growth. As of 1950, the level of real product per capita in the United States was approximately twice that of Western Europe, on average. Since World War II, however, the situation has been reversed. From 1950 to 1959, rates of increase in real product per year worked in the United States were well below the average of the countries shown in part A of table 6.1. For the 1960–75 period, we must shift to comparisons of rates of change in output per hour in manufacturing shown in part B of the table. There, we again see that the

Table 6.1. Recent and Long-Term Growth Rates in Real National Product per Year Worked and Output per Hour in Manufacturing, Thirteen Countries

(average annual percentage rates of change)

Country	(A) Real National Product per Year Worked			(B) Output per Hour in Manufacturing 1960–75
	Starting Year	To 1959	1950–59	
Japan	1880	2.9	6.1	9.7
Italy	1863	1.2	4.7	6.2
Germany	1853	1.5	4.5	5.7
France	1855	1.5	3.6	5.6
Netherlands	1900	1.1	3.4	7.1
Norway	1865	1.6	3.1	n.a.
Sweden	1863	2.1	2.8	6.6
United States	1871	2.0	2.2	2.7
Canada	1872	1.7	2.0	4.0
Denmark	1872	1.6	1.8	7.2
United Kingdom	1857	1.2	1.7	3.8
Belgium	—	n.a.	n.a.	7.0
Switzerland	—	n.a.	n.a.	5.1

n.a. = not available.

SOURCES: For real national product—Deborah C. Paige, et al., "Economic Growth: The Last Hundred Years," National Institute of Economic and Social Research, *Economic Review,* July 1961, p. 69; for output—Arthur Neef, "Unit Labor Costs in Eleven Countries," U.S. Department of Labor, *Monthly Labor Review,* August 1971, p. 4.

rate of advance in all of the other ten countries exceeded that in the United States.

These results are not surprising. The relative gains abroad particularly for West Germany, Japan, and Italy, were due in part to recovery from the extensive destruction of World War II. The United States aided significantly in this recovery. Though not shown in the table, the Soviet Union also exhibited relatively high rates of productivity increase in the 1950s, followed by slower rates in the 1960s.

More fundamentally, the relatively high rates of productivity advance abroad resulted from a conscious and determined effort to catch up with the more advanced technology and management practices in the United States. Not only were the West European nations and Japan determined to reduce the technology gap, but we in fact helped them do so by our foreign aid and investment programs, especially through direct investment abroad by U.S. multinational corporations, which provided know-how as well as new plants and equipment. Although other countries were developing some new products and technology, much of their progress was the result of borrowing and adapting more advanced U.S. technology to their requirements. Doing so necessitated high levels of saving and investment within these countries, promoted by special tax advantages and subsidies granted by their governments. The creation of the European Economic Community and a gradual reduction of trade barriers in general helped expand the size of markets and hence the size of establishments and firms in those countries, and there were attendant economies in production.

Edward F. Denison put considerable stress not only on economies of scale but also on structural changes in the West European economies as a reason for accelerated productivity growth.[1] In particular, the shifts of employment out of agriculture and self-employment into nonagricultural employment, where value added per person is higher, contributed significantly more to productivity advance in Europe than in the United States. Although Denison attributed more than half of the productivity difference between the United States and Europe (about 40 percent in 1960) to the lower level of technological knowledge in Europe, he estimated that advances in knowledge proceeded at about the same pace in both areas, at least during the period from 1950 to 1962. His estimates confirm, however, that the growth of real productive capital per person employed was substantially faster in Western Europe and Japan than in the United States.

Reliable productivity estimates are not available for most of the less developed countries (LDCs), particularly those in Asia, Africa, and Latin America. Fragmentary data suggest that some of these countries, such as Taiwan, Israel, and Mexico, are increasing productivity and per capita income at a faster rate than the United States. Others, despite aid from the United Nations and from the United States and other countries, have apparently not yet taken off into a significant rate of economic growth. However, the fact that some of the LDCs have narrowed the per capita income gap between themselves and the advanced nations is a hopeful sign for the future.

Productivity and Comparative Changes in Costs and Prices

International differences in productivity changes are an important element in relative changes in prices, but they are not the whole story. The change in labor costs per unit of output is in proportion to the percentage changes in average hourly labor compensation, less the percentage change in output per hour. This relationship largely explains price trends, since nonlabor costs are a fairly steady proportion of total costs over longer periods of time.

Thus, if average hour earnings in all countries showed the same rates of increase, relative unit labor costs would vary *inversely* with relative changes in labor productivity. In reality, changes in *both* average hourly earnings and productivity vary among countries, so that relative changes in unit labor costs (and prices) reflect both variables, as is demonstrated in table 6.2.

The 1970–75 period, shown in the table, was a period of slowing growth in productivity. Output growth was also slowing in the United States and most other countries because of

Table 6.2. Comparative Rates of Change in Productivity, Average Earnings,
and Unit Labor Costs, Twelve Countries, 1970–75

(average annual percentage rates of change)

Country	Output per Hour	Average Hourly Compensation	Unit Labor Costs National Currency	Unit Labor Costs U.S. Dollars
United States	1.8	8.0	6.1	6.1
Canada	2.7	10.0	7.1	7.8
Japan	5.4	20.7	14.5	19.8
Belgium	7.6	16.9	8.7	16.1
Denmark	6.8	15.5	8.1	14.7
France	3.4	15.1	11.4	17.3
West Germany	5.4	13.3	7.5	17.3
Italy	6.0	22.1	15.2	14.0
Netherlands	5.8	16.0	9.7	18.6
Sweden	5.0	14.1	8.7	13.9
Switzerland	3.5	11.9	8.2	20.3
United Kingdom	3.1	16.4	12.9	11.2

SOURCE: U.S. Department of Labor, Bureau of Labor Statistics.

capacity limits reached by 1973, the oil embargo that began in the fall of 1973 and lasted well into 1974, and the world-wide economic contraction in 1974 and 1975. Since 1970 was also a recession year, the 1970–75 comparison still provides an approximate picture of relative trends.

On average, from 1970 through 1975, the rate of manufacturing productivity advance in the United States, 1.8 percent a year, continued well below the eleven-country average. The lowest rates among the others were recorded by Canada, 2.7 percent and the United Kingdom, 3.1 percent. The highest rate was that of Belguim, 7.6 percent.

But average hourly compensation went up less in the United States than in any other country between 1970 and 1975, as shown in the table. The 8.0 percent average annual rate of increase compares with double-digit rates in the eleven other countries—Japan and Italy registered increases averaging over 20 percent a year. The relative increases abroad were more than enough to offset their advantage in productivity growth. Consequently, unit labor costs in U.S. manufacturing rose less than in any other country between 1970 and 1975—at a 6.1 percent average annual rate, compared with an average of more than 9 percent for the others as measured in national currencies. Because of the devaluations of the dollar during this period, the increases abroad as measured in U.S. dollars were considerably greater. It was this relative improvement in U.S. unit labor costs and prices that reversed the deterioration of the U.S. balance of payments and contributed to a substantial surplus in the balance of trade in 1975.

Between 1974 and 1975, productivity in U.S. manufacturing dropped by 0.7 percent, and it either dropped or decelerated sharply in the other countries, reflecting the world-wide economic contraction. Yet average hourly compensation actually accelerated or continued to rise at high rates, as organized labor sought to catch up with the inflationary surge of 1973 and 1974. Unit labor costs, in national currencies, continued to rise faster abroad than in the United States in 1975 with the exception of West Germany, which had been able to continue to increase productivity while bringing down the rate of increase in average hourly compensation. Under the floating exchange rate system, the pattern of relative changes in unit labor costs measured in U.S. dollars deviated somewhat from the pattern reflecting changes in national currencies. Thus, in U.S. dollars unit labor costs in Germany rose more than in the U.S. as a result of appreciation of the mark, but they rose less in Canada because of depreciation of the Canadian dollar vis-à-vis the U.S. dollar.

In the 1975–76 recovery, productivity rose smartly in the United States, at about 6.5 percent in manufacturing. It presumably rose in other economies as well, although estimates for other countries were not yet available at the time of writing. Further, rates of increase in average hourly compensation decelerated somewhat, reflecting above-average unemployment and considerable disinflation. As a result, unit labor costs decelerated sharply to a 0.9 percent rate in the United States, even more than the deceleration in price inflation. Although figures for other countries are not yet available, it may be inferred that generally the deceleration in unit labor costs was not as great as in the United States, since prices abroad were generally still rising faster than in the United States during 1976.

Since productivity changes, together with changes in labor and other factor prices, underlie movements in general price levels, they also affect exchange rates under a system of floating exchange rates. Yet exchange rates reflect not only relative price movements in various countries but also financial flows. Therefore, in the real world there is only a tenuous link between relative productivity changes and changes in exchange rates. In a fundamental sense, however, after taking account of exchange rate changes, the currencies of nations achieving higher-than-average productivity increases tend to gain in terms of purchasing power over the products of countries with lower productivity gains.

Cross-Country Industry Productivity Comparisons

In basic economics we are taught that international trade depends on comparative costs. That is, if the price of a given commodity in country A is enough lower relative to the country's general price level than its relative price is in country B, then country B will tend to import the commodity from country A. And imports tend to increase if the relative price of a commodity in country A is falling in comparison with its relative price in country B.

From the analysis in chapter 5, we know that relative price movements are negatively correlated with relative productivity movements. Therefore, relative productivity movements in different countries, through their effects on prices, affect patterns of international trade. Note, however, that—since floating exchange rates tend to equalize the purchasing power of currencies over internationally traded goods and services—it is the movements of prices of given products in various countries *relative* to the general price levels that are significant.

For an example of differences in relative productivity movements, look at the indexes for the iron and steel industry in five countries in table 6.3. During the period covered (1964–73), productivity advanced much more rapidly in Japan, West Germany, and France than in the United States and the United

Table 6.3. Relative Output per Hour, Hourly Labor Costs, and Unit Labor Costs in the Iron and Steel Industries, Five Countries, 1964–73

(U.S.=100)

	Output per hour		Hourly labor cost in U.S. dollars				Unit labor cost in U.S. dollars			
			Constant 1964 exchange rates		Current exchange rates		Constant 1964 exchange rates		Current exchange rates	
	Mini-mum	Maxi-mum	Mini-mum	Maxi-mum	Mini-mum	Maxi-mum	Mini-mum	Maxi-mum	Mini-mum	Maxi-mum
Each Year	100	100	100	100	100	100	100	100	100	100
United States										
Japan										
1964	43	54	17	17	17	17	31	40	31	40
1965	43	54	18	19	18	19	34	43	34	43
1966	51	63	20	20	20	20	31	39	31	39
1967	63	78	21	22	21	22	27	35	27	35
1968	68	85	23	24	23	24	27	35	28	35
1969	83	103	26	26	26	26	25	32	25	32
1970	97	120	30	30	30	30	25	31	25	32
1971	94	116	31	31	32	33	26	34	28	35
1972	102	127	30	31	36	37	24	30	29	36
1973	117	146	35	35	47	47	24	30	32	40
France										
1964	48	51	34	35	34	35	66	72	66	72
1965	48	52	35	36	36	37	69	75	69	75
1966	50	54	36	37	36	37	67	73	67	73
1967	55	59	37	38	37	38	63	68	63	68
1968	59	63	39	40	39	40	63	68	62	67
1969	64	69	41	41	38	39	59	64	56	61
1970	68	72	44	45	39	40	61	66	54	59
1971	65	69	46	47	41	42	67	73	60	65
1972	66	71	48	49	46	47	68	73	66	71

(U.S.=100)

	Hourly labor cost in U.S. dollars						Unit labor cost in U.S. dollars			
	Output per hour		Constant 1964 exchange rates		Current exchange rates		Constant 1964 exchange rates		Current exchange rates	
	Mini-mum	Maxi-mum	Mini-mum	Maxi-mum	Mini-mum	Maxi-mum	Mini-mum	Maxi-mum	Mini-mum	Maxi-mum
West Germany										
1964	54	63	37	39	37	39	58	72	58	72
1965	52	61	38	40	38	40	62	77	62	77
1966	52	61	39	42	39	42	64	79	64	79
1967	59	69	39	42	39	42	56	70	56	70
1968	65	75	39	41	39	41	52	64	52	64
1969	71	83	40	43	41	43	49	60	49	61
1970	72	84	47	51	52	55	57	70	62	77
1971	69	80	48	52	55	59	60	75	69	85
1972	72	84	47	50	58	62	56	69	70	86
1973	72	84	48	52	73	78	58	72	87	197
United Kingdom										
1964	46	50	29	30	29	30	57	64	57	64
1965	47	51	31	32	31	32	61	68	61	68
1966	45	48	32	33	32	33	67	75	67	75
1967	46	50	30	31	30	31	61	68	60	67
1968	48	52	32	33	27	28	61	69	53	59
1969	49	53	32	33	28	29	61	68	52	58
1970	51	55	35	37	30	31	64	72	55	62
1971	47	51	35	36	31	32	69	77	60	67
1972	49	53	37	38	33	34	69	77	62	69
1973	47	51	39	40	34	35	76	85	67	75

SOURCE: Bureau of Labor Statistics, U.S. Department of Labor.

Kingdom. In 1964 output per hour was about 60 percent of the U.S. level in Germany and about 50 percent in the other three countries. By 1973, although labor productivity in the British steel industry was still only about half that in the United States, the French industry was up to two-thirds and the German to about three-fourths; the Japanese had exceeded the average level in the United States.

Although the table does not show index numbers of productivity in each of the economies as a whole, we know that productivity in the U.S. steel industry rose less than in the private economy as a whole (thus declined relatively), whereas productivity in the Japanese, German, and French industries rose relatively. Therefore, prices of steel-mill products in those three countries fell relatively, while in the United States they rose relatively. As a result, net imports of steel into the United States increased substantially over the years, until a voluntary quota arrangement was worked out in 1971 to limit foreign imports.

The basic oxygen furnace was a major cost-reducing innovation in the steel industry. Between 1960 and 1970 both Germany and Japan increased the proportion of steel produced in such furnaces considerably faster than did the U.S. industry. This was not true of France; but there were, of course, other innovations, such as the continuous casting process that affected productivity.

It is a fair bet that, if productivity estimates were available for certain other industries in foreign countries, such as textiles and footware, they would show relative increases in contrast to relative declines in the United States. This can be inferred from the fact that relative prices for these products have risen in the United States, which has led to increases in imports and to declining international competitiveness of the domestic industries. These are the industries whose spokesmen are in the forefront of those calling for increased protection of American production and, they allege, of jobs.

It should be remembered, however, that as we increase our imports from other countries, their dollar earnings rise, increasing demand for U.S. exports. This benefits those of our industries whose relative productivity is increasing and whose relative prices are decreasing in relation to the relative movements abroad. Such a comparative advantage is enjoyed by most of our high-technology industries. Examples are the machine tool and computer industries, in which the rates of innovation are higher in the United States than in our major trading partners.

In general, the U.S. net trade balance in high-technology, R-&-D-intensive products has risen in recent years. The net trade balance in non-R-&-D-intensive products has fallen since 1964 and became seriously negative by the early 1970s. This is a reason for additional concern about the declining ratio of R & D to GNP in the United States, in comparison with rising ratios in other major nations.

The basic approach for firms in industries whose comparative productivity is lagging relative to foreign competition is to try to improve their rate of productivity advance. In chapter 11, we discuss methods by which companies have tried to increase their productivity. It is a fact of economic life, however, that no country can increase its comparative productivity performance in all industries. There will always be some industries that have declining net exports or rising net imports, which will drive the less efficient firms of the industry out of business and possibly reduce employment in that industry. But rather than protect less efficient industries, most economists would prefer to see the government help ease the adjustment problems of the affected companies and workers, as discussed in chapter 10. Planes of living throughout the world will rise more rapidly if resources are permitted to shift in accord with present or potential comparative productivity and cost advantages—with the possible exception of industries in which there is a vital national security interest.

7

Causal Forces Behind Productivity Advance

Understanding the causes of productivity increase is a necessary background for the conscious formulation of policies to facilitate and promote economic progress. In this chapter we first discuss causal forces in general terms: short-run forces, often associated with the business cycle; long-term proximate factors, particularly investments required for cost-reducing technological progress; and finally, underlying factors associated with basic values and the legal and institutional framework of an economy. After the general discussion we shall summarize the results of some recent empirical studies that have tried to quantify the effects of some of the forces involved in productivity growth.

Short-Term Factors

Changes in rates of utilization of capacity of individual plants, industries, and sectors away from or toward the most efficient rates obviously affect rates of productivity change. This is largely a cyclical phenomenon, but differences in average rates of utilization between successive business cycle peaks would also have some effect on subperiod rates of change. The effect on long-run trends would be minor.

Also in the short run, change in degree of efficiency of production relative to the potential efficiency with a given technology would affect productivity change. In the case of relatively new technologies the steepness of the learning curve —that is, the rapidity with which the requirements of a new technology are learned by individuals or groups, refined, and integrated in organization routines—affects productivity. In this regard, investments in training and retraining are a factor. Even in the case of older technologies the degree of labor efficiency, relative to realizable standards or norms, affects productivity. Changes in efficiency, so defined, as revealed by work measurement, also depend on motivation factors, given the institutional framework. Labor efficiency, like utilization rates, seems to have a systematic cyclical component; that is, productivity rises before the trough, as the profit squeeze increases managements' cost-consciousness and as rising unemployment motivates workers to value their jobs more highly and work more productively. The reverse of these factors may help to account for the slowdown of productivity gains before cycle peaks.

Finally, since innovations and their diffusion usually require investment and since investment is notoriously cyclical, so also is innovation. But the effect on productivity may be obscured by other factors. For example, whereas a decline in the rate of tangible investment will retard the growth in efficiency of the existing capital stock (as its average age increases), the tendency to concentrate production in newer, more efficient plants during a recession would help raise productivity. Similarly, the tendency to upgrade the employed labor force in a contraction would obscure a retardation in growth of quality of the total labor force as human investment declined. The opposite tendencies would appear in an economic expansion.

Secular Forces

Productivity advance is not a magical touchstone that raises output more than inputs at no cost. Indeed, the technological advances that reduce unit real costs and raise productivity usually require investments to create the new knowledge and know-how and to incorporate them in human beings and in nonhuman productive agents. There also are non-investment-related forces that affect productivity, which we shall enumerate after discussing the more important investment categories associated with technological progress.

Investments

All outlays that contribute to output- and income-producing capacity (capital) for future periods may be defined broadly as investment. This definition does not only include the outlays for tangible structures, equipment, inventories, and development of natural resources, which are traditionally considered to represent capital formation; by analogy, it could also include the cost of rearing children to working age, that is, the formation of tangible human capital. But it is the intangible investments designed to improve the quality and efficiency of the tangible nonhuman and human factors that are of particular significance in explaining productivity advance.

The fountainhead of technological progress is basic research, which increases human knowledge. On the one hand, basic research feeds into and draws from applied research, development, and engineering designed to develop new products (including cost-reducing goods for producers) and new processes. Thus, new technology becomes embodied in producers' goods and processes and is diffused through tangible investments in successive generations ("vintages") of capital goods. Note that, as a carrier of technological progress, the rate of tangible investment is important. If the rate increases and the average age of durable capital declines, this contributes to an acceleration in the rate of productivity advance, and vice versa.

On the other hand, both basic and applied research feed into and draw from education and training. The advances in knowledge and know-how increase the content and quality of curricula. Increases in both the quantity (years of schooling) and the quality of education and training per worker are necessary to enable the labor force to initiate and adapt to an increasingly complex technology. Likewise, investments in medical care, health, and safety enhance the quantity and quality of human inputs by prolonging working life, reducing time lost due to illness and accident, and increasing vitality as chronic and debilitating conditions are overcome.

Actually, it is the growth of the stocks of the intangible capital embodied in the work force and in the nonhuman tangible capital goods, relative to the quantities of the latter (unadjusted for quality), that would be expected to increase productivity. Also, it is the advances in technological knowledge resulting from research and development that render economic the increasing intensities of investments per worker and per hour by raising the prospective rates of return.

Other Proximate Forces

There are several non-investment-related forces that directly affect productivity. First, there are internal and external economies of scale. There are the opportunities opened up by growth of markets for greater specialization of personnel, machines, and plants, and the spreading of overhead functions over more units. Technological progress helps extend the frontiers of optimum scale, so that this force continues operative even after substantial growth. It should also be noted that potentials for scale economies frequently require investments for realization.

The second major factor is change in the degree of economic efficiency—that is, allocation of resources in accord with the community's preferences. Perhaps the ideal model is that of the perfectly competitive economy, in which knowledge is complete and changes therefore are adjusted to instantaneously. Actually, monopolistic and restrictive practices by managements and labor unions—and market interventions by governments—create distortions in the allocation of resources. Thus, changes in institutional forces and practices can affect productivity. Further, the market is not perfect; so the mix of investments and capital and the distribution of the labor force generally are suboptimal. The problem is compounded by the frictions and lags in adjusting factor supplies to changes in relative demand that result from changes in technology and other dynamic forces. Thus, more rapid adjustments to change could raise productivity. To some degree, this may involve investments in market research in the case of capital and in physical mobility in the case of labor.

Finally, there may be changes in the average inherent quality of natural and human resources (there is no inherent quality of man-made capital goods), not counting changes in quality due to investment. The tendency toward diminishing returns in extractive industries is an old "law" whose relevance has been recognized anew in recent years. In the case of labor, average quality may change as a result of changing mix of groups (particularly age-brackets) that have different productivities, as reflected in earning capacities. Or, if one is looking at labor input, changes in the quality of an hour's work of a given type due to changes in the length of the workyear could be included under this rubric.

Basic Values and Institutions

The basic value system of a society, which conditions its institutions and practices, obviously has an important bearing on productivity. Attitudes and ambitions of individuals with regard to increasing their real incomes and economic status; propensities to save, invest, and incur risks; willingness to adapt to change—all of these have a bearing on potential rates of productivity advance. More specific attitudes of individuals toward their work, the organizations in which they work, and toward the economic system in general also affect their efficiency.

Interacting with the basic values of people are their institutional forms and practices. Institutions are created and evolve within a set of laws and governmental regulations, of course. The legal framework and changes in laws and regulations are particularly important, for they govern the rewards for high and rising productivity and the penalties for subnormal performance. In a mixed economy, such as ours for example, several kinds of factors have significant impacts on productivity: the rules for the competitive sector and policing under the antitrust laws; the modes of regulating public utilities and other natural monopolies; the nature of interventions in the operation of markets; and social legislation and regulations, among others.

Further, in an economy with a substantial private enterprise sector, the actions of the central government in managing macroeconomic policies—fiscal, monetary, and incomes—will have an important effect on productivity, particularly through their impact on after-tax income. For after-tax rates of return are a major factor influencing investment, both as an incentive and as a source of funds, since, as we have seen, investment is the chief proximate determinant of productivity trends.

Explanations of Recent Productivity Trends

It is difficult to quantify the effects of the various causal forces on productivity change. Even if all the significant forces can be identified and measured, it is still hard to disentangle the effects of the several interacting variables; for example, technological advance resulting from research and development creates demand for more professional personnel and thus for educational investment. Despite the difficulties, a number of economists have tried to narrow the productivity residual by measuring the effects of some of the causal forces. All of the investigators are still left with a final residual, however, which reflects the net effect of all of the factors not explicitly included in the explanatory schema.

In my earlier work, I weighted hours worked and capital inputs by average compensation in terms of about thirty industry groupings. Relative shifts of resources toward industries with higher average pay and higher returns resulted in weighted factor inputs rising about 0.3 percentage point more than unweighted inputs (or about 15 percent of the residual).

Dale Jorgenson has followed a more elaborate weighting scheme.[1] For labor, he measured input in terms not only of industries, but also of sex, race, and occupational and educational class. His weighted labor input rose by 0.8 percentage point more than the unweighted in the 1947–73 period, and he took this as a measure of labor quality improvement. His capital input index, weighted by average rental rates in sixty-five industry groupings, rose by 1.2 percentage points more than the unweighted measure. His total factor quality measure rose by about one percentage point, which explains over 40 percent of the difference between the 4.2 and 1.9 average annual percentage rates of increase in real product and unadjusted total factor input.

I obtained a similar result in a study for the National Bureau of Economic Research, using a different approach.[2] I estimated the real stock of capital resulting from investments designed to increase the efficiency, or "quality," of the factors of production. These comprised research and development, education and training, and health and mobility. The total real stock of capital, human and nonhuman, including the intangible stocks associated with rising quality, grew by 0.8 percentage point a year more than the real unadjusted stock from 1948 to 1969. Again, this represented something over 40 percent of the productivity residual, that is, the difference between rates of growth of real product and real stocks of labor and capital, unadjusted for quality. This computation assumes the save average rate of return on intangible investment as on tangible. There is some evidence that the rate of return on intangible investment has been higher, in which case the contribution of quality improvements associated with technological and organizational progress would be higher.

Perhaps the most painstaking and comprehensive effort to partition economic growth in general, and productivity increase in particular, among causal forces is that by Edward F. Denison.[3] His analysis of sources is shown in table 7.1, rearranged slightly for comparability with my approach. Denison includes changes in the quality of labor as part of labor input, so his productivity estimate is correspondingly lower. In the table I also show the quantity of labor input separately and a productivity variable that relates real product to combined quantities of capital (including land) and labor, unadjusted for quality. This productivity variable shows an average annual rate of increase of 2.68 percent between 1948 and 1969, compared with my estimate of 2.6 percent when inputs are not weighted by industry.

Denison estimates that the increase in labor quality accounts for 0.54 percentage point of the growth rate, or about 22 percent of the rate of productivity advance. Including labor quality with input, Denison's rate of productivity advance is 2.14. The increase in labor quality was due largely to the effects of in-

Table 7.1. Components of Economic Growth, U.S. Nonresidential Business Economy (percentage distribution)

	1948–69	1964–69
Real sector income	3.72	4.52
Labor input, quantity	0.46	1.84
Employment	0.84	2.13
Average hours worked	−0.38	−0.29
Labor input, quality	0.54	0.36
Efficiency per hour	0.05	0.12
Intergroup shifts	0.11	0.13
Age-sex composition	−0.12	−0.38
Education	0.50	0.49
Capital inputs, quantity	0.58	0.78
Output per unit of input		
Excluding labor in quality changes	2.68	2.15
Including labor quality changes	2.14	1.79
Advances in knowledge and n.e.c.	1.44	1.43
Improved resource allocation	0.37	0.42
Economies of scale	0.51	0.68
Irregular factors (especially demand intensity)	−0.18	−0.74

n.e.c. = not elsewhere classified.

SOURCE: Adapted from Edward F. Denison, *Accounting for United States Growth, 1929-1969*, Tables 8–2 and 8–5.

creased education, as in Jorgenson's estimate. Shifts in age-sex composition toward groups with lower earnings, particularly in the latter 1960s, had a 0.12 negative effect. But this was offset by the positive effect of other intergroup shifts. There was a small positive effect in the efficiency of an average hour's work as a result of the downward trend in the average length of the workweek and workyear.

Also explaining almost 20 percent of the broader productivity change measure were economies of scale in both local and national markets. This factor is, of course, related to the overall rate of economic growth. Over the 1948–69 period it was, however, partly offset by the effect of a decrease in the intensity of demand relative to capacity. Improved resource allocation accounted for about 13 percent of the productivity gain. It was due chiefly to the continuing relative shift of resources out of farming, but the change also reflects the relative decline of nonfarm self-employment.

Finally, the residual, which Denison interprets as predominantly reflecting advances in knowledge, comprises slightly more than half of the rate of productivity increase. Since Denison does not separately measure improvements in the quality of capital, his residual reflects the advances in knowledge embodied in plants, equipment, and developed land. It also reflects the higher quality of education and training as advances in knowledge improve the corpus transmitted, although Denison's labor quality does capture increases in the average amount of education per worker. Presumably, most of the advances in knowledge in the modern era stem from investments in research and development, although informal scientific and inventive activities are not inconsequential.

8
Productivity, Costs, and Prices

Up to this point, we have stated that increases in the real income of labor and owners of nonhuman factors depend on increases in productivity. But we have not explained the price mechanisms whereby productivity gains are distributed to the factors. Actually, there is a unique relationship between changes in factor prices and in product prices, based on productivity changes, that explains the growth in real incomes of the factors. And differences in the rates of change in average hourly labor compensation and in the prices of capital (including land) are an important element in explaining changes in the distribution of national income between labor and property. Further, the relation between prices of factor services and of products is an important facet of the inflationary process, which underlies past attempts to establish wage-price guideposts or incomes policies. We shall examine these matters in the first section of this chapter, with particular reference to time periods comprising two or more business cycles.

During business cycles in the United States there has been a typical pattern of relative movements of factor prices, productivity, unit costs, and product prices, which we shall summarize in the second section of this chapter. As suggested in chapter 4, these relationships form an important part of the explanation for economic fluctuations. Since economic contractions, with the attendant increases in unemployment rates, have a disruptive effect on labor markets, it is appropriate that we investigate the role of productivity changes in the cycle mechanism.

Long-Run Trends

It is a truism that the average price of labor and capital services combined rises faster than the average price of final products (excluding indirect taxes) in proportion to the rate of increase in total factor productivity. This relationship can be easily demonstrated if the reader will bear with a little algebra. First, recall that national income equals national product when indirect business taxes less subsidies are subtracted from product, so that it equals the gross factor costs required to produce it. Call national income and product Y. When national product is deflated (divided) by average product prices (P_O), real product, or final output (O), is obtained. When national income (which equals factor cost) is divided by the average price of inputs (P_I), real factor cost, or input (I), is obtained. Thus, total factor productivity (O/I) can be viewed as the ratio of factor input prices to product prices:

$$\frac{O}{I} = \frac{Y}{P_O} \div \frac{Y}{P_I} = \frac{P_I}{P_O}$$

Therefore, changes in the ratio of input prices to output prices must be proportional to changes in total factor productivity. In view of the income-product identity, real income per unit of the factors increases in proportion to productivity. If labor or property-owners seek to increase real incomes by raising money incomes faster than productivity, increases in prices inevitably cut their total money income gains back in line with productivity increases in terms of purchasing power.

This can be illustrated by numbers for the 1948–66 period (before the inflationary upsurge of the past decade). Average prices of factor inputs in the private domestic business economy rose at an average annual rate of 3.9 percent, while average product prices (the "implicit deflator" for GNP originating in the sector) rose at an average rate of 1.4 percent a year. The reconciliation between the two numbers is provided by a 2.5 percent annual rate of increase in total factor productivity (3.9 minus 1.4).[1]

There are some interesting implications of this identity. For one thing, it is obvious that in order to have a stable general price level (Po), average input prices must rise no more than in proportion to total factor productivity. When they do, it is of course no proof of cost-push inflation. Even if increases in aggregate demand are outrunning increases in supply and pulling product prices up, input prices will still rise by more in proportion to productivity. This is because demand-pull inflation first acts to raise profit margins, which are reflected in the factor price measures, and subsequently tends to accelerate increases in wage-rates, the major component of factor prices. In other periods, however, when demand-pull is not evident, as indicated by excess capacity and stable or falling profit margins, an increase in factor prices (predominantly wage-rates) greater than the rise in productivity is generally viewed as evidence of cost-push.

The productivity-cost-price relationship underlay the wage-price guideposts formulated in 1962 by the Council of Economic Advisers (CEA), which for several years were effective in restraining price inflation. It has necessarily been a consideration in subsequent experiments with incomes policies, so called because attempts to influence prices of factors and products obviously affect incomes. The CEA approach was through the price of labor (average hourly compensation) and labor productivity (real product per hour), chiefly because federal statistical agencies do not estimate total factor prices and productivity. Also, the labor approach is easier to understand, and in any case labor constitutes more than three-quarters of total net factor cost if imputed labor earnings of proprietors are included.

The CEA guidepost for noninflationary wage increases was the trend-rate of increase in real private product per hour, then computed to average 3.2 percent a year. That is, a 3.2 percent increase in average hourly compensation would be offset by a 3.2 percent decrease in hours required to produce a unit of output, so that total labor costs per unit of output would remain constant. Under these conditions, average prices would also remain constant, assuming that nonlabor costs (interest, rents, and profits) remained a constant fraction of total factor costs, which is roughly the case over the long run.

The CEA noted that 3.2 percent was the guidepost for *average* wage increases. In labor markets where relative demand was rising, it was recognized that above-average wage increases would be needed to elicit the necessary supply, and vice versa for markets in which the relative demand for labor was falling. Even more important, it was recognized that industries differ widely in rates of productivity change. The CEA explicitly stated that, in industries with above-average productivity gains, price decreases would be expected. Conversely, in industries with below-average productivity gains, price increases would be in order. This guideline conforms to the historical experience, as we saw in chapter 5, with respect to relative industry changes in productivity and prices.

Considering the difficulty of working with averages in diverse industry situations, the CEA guideposts worked reasonably well in holding inflation to modest proportions, aided by cushions of unused capacity in the economy. But by late 1965, when increasing deficit spending was resorted to for financing U.S. involvement in Southeast Asia, demand-pull inflation rendered the guideposts ineffective.

In 1971, wage-price controls followed an initial wage-price freeze of ninety days. Under Phase 2, price increases were granted companies by the Price Commission only if they could be cost-justified—that is, firms had to demonstrate statistically that their labor costs, with due allowance for labor productivity gains, and their other costs per unit of product, had risen as much over a past period as their requested price increase. Actually, an incentive was built into the price control regulations to spur firms to accelerate their productivity increases in order to realize an increase in profit margins.

Before leaving the productivity-cost-price relation, let us go back and see what happened over the 1948–66 period in terms of both the labor and capital factors. According to my computations, real product per hour increased at an average annual rate of 3.1 percent between 1948 and 1966 in the private domestic business economy. This is consistent with the 3.2 percent CEA guidepost, which was based on a shorter time period and a broader segment of the economy, including households and private nonprofit institutions. Over the same period, average hourly labor compensation rose by 4.7 percent a year, on average. Thus, labor cost per unit of output rose at an average annual rate of 1.6 percent (4.7 minus 3.1). The general price level, as measured by the implicit price deflator for gross product, rose somewhat less—by 1.4 percent a year. This was possible because unit property costs increased at an average annual rate of only 0.8 percent a year. The 0.8 percent is the difference between the average annual rates of increase in the price of capital, 1.3 percent, and in capital productivity, 0.5 percent. The price of capital reflects changes in two main variables: the price of capital goods, which rose at much the same rate as the general price level; and the rate of return on property, which sagged slightly, by less than 0.1 percent a year on average. The increase in the implicit price deflator is the weighted average of each of the two unit factor cost changes: labor, at 1.6 percent (weighted about 0.75) and capital, at 0.8 percent (weighted about 0.25).

The CEA guidepost was a good rough guide to noninflationary wage-rate increases. But it was not exact, since it did not take unit capital costs into account in a precise way. Instead of remaining a constant fraction of total factor costs, capital costs (income) actually declined somewhat—form 30.3 percent in 1948 to 27.5 percent in 1966. This happens when capital productivity rises but the rate of return remains relatively constant—which it tends to do over the long run—or if the rate of return drops.

The rising share of labor in national income is also reflected in the movement of *real* average hourly labor compensation, which rose at a 3.3 percent average annual rate (4.7 percent gain in money terms, less the 1.4 percent increase in the price deflator). This was 0.2 percent more than the 3.1 percent rate of increase in labor productivity; and 0.2 percent was also the rate of increase in the labor share of national income. It was made possible by the 0.6 percent difference between the 0.5 percent a year increase in capital productivity and the 0.1 percent a year drop in the real price of capital.

Thus, under average trend conditions, the noninflationary wage increase can exceed the rate of increase in real product per hour by a small margin. But in general, the trend in real average hourly earnings is very close to the trend in output per hour (see figures 8.1 and 8.2). The trend for the entire 1947–75 period is pictured in figure 8.1. As indicated by the underlying numbers in table 8.1 and 8.2, the average annual percentage rate of increase for both real average hourly compensation and

Figure 8.1. Output per Hour and Real Compensation per Hour: Private Business Sector, 1945–75

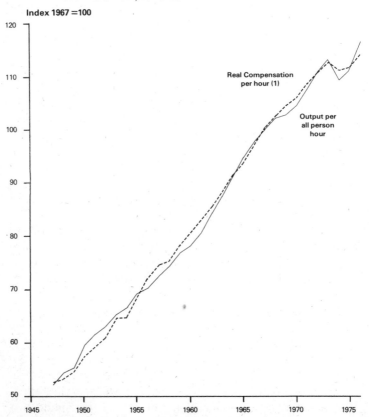

1. Compensation per hour deflated by the implicit price deflator for the private business sector.

SOURCE: Department of Labor, Bureau of Labor Statistics.

Figure 8.2. Compensation per Hour, Unit Labor Costs, and Prices: Private Business Sector, 1945–75

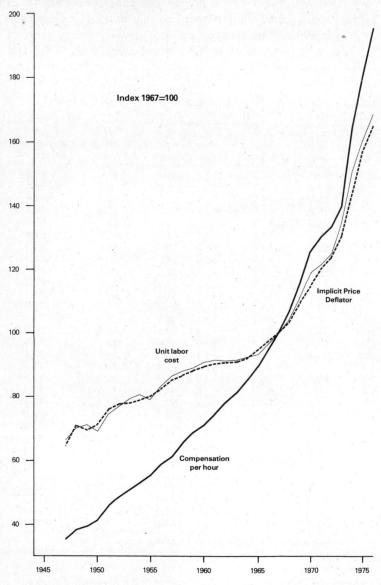

Index 1967=100

Unit labor cost

Implicit Price Deflator

Compensation per hour

SOURCE: Department of Labor, Bureau of Labor Statistics.

output per hour was 2.8 percent. The charts and tables also show that nominal average hourly compensation rose at an average annual rate of 6.1 percent so that unit labor costs rose by 3.2 percent a year, on average. The almost parallel average increase in the price level of 3.3 percent a year (figure 8.2 and

Table 8.1. Productivity and Costs: U.S. Private Business Sector, 1947-76
(Index 1967=100)

Year	Output per All Person Hour	Compensation per Hour	Unit Labor Cost	Implicit Price Deflator	Real Compensation per Hour[a]	Real Compensation per Hour[b]
1947	52.3	35.1	67.1	65.1	52.5	53.9
1948	54.4	38.1	70.1	70.6	53.0	54.0
1949	55.3	38.8	70.2	69.8	54.4	55.6
1950	59.7	41.6	69.6	70.8	57.7	58.8
1951	61.5	45.6	74.3	76.0	58.7	60.0
1952	63.0	48.6	77.1	77.4	61.0	62.8
1953	65.3	51.8	79.3	77.9	64.6	66.5
1954	66.5	53.5	80.5	78.6	66.5	68.1
1955	69.2	54.9	79.3	79.8	68.5	68.8
1956	70.2	58.6	83.5	82.2	72.0	71.3
1957	72.3	62.5	86.5	84.8	74.3	73.7
1958	74.2	65.5	88.2	86.4	75.6	75.8
1959	76.8	68.5	89.1	88.1	78.3	77.8
1960	78.1	71.4	91.4	89.3	80.5	80.0
1961	80.6	74.2	92.1	89.8	83.0	82.6
1962	84.4	77.7	92.1	90.6	85.7	85.8
1963	87.7	80.7	92.0	91.4	88.1	88.3
1964	91.3	85.1	93.2	92.7	91.5	91.8
1965	94.7	88.4	93.4	94.2	93.6	93.8
1966	97.8	94 7	96.8	97.2	97.3	97.4
1967	100.0	100.0	100.0	100.0	100.0	100.0
1968	103.3	107.6	104.1	103.9	103.9	103.6
1969	103.7	115.1	111.0	108.8	104.6	105.8
1970	104.5	123.3	118.1	113.9	106.0	108.3
1971	107.8	131.5	121.9	118.9	108.2	110.6
1972	110.9	138.9	125.2	123.2	110.8	112.7
1973	113.1	150.3	132.9	130.3	112.8	115.3
1974	109.2	164.3	150.4	143.8	111.1	114.3
1975	111.5	180.2	161.6	157.5	111.8	114.4
1976	116.4	195.0	167.4	164.6	114.3	118.5

a. Compensation deflated by Consumer Price Index.
b. Compensation deflated by the implicit price deflator for private business sector.

SOURCE: Department of Labor, Bureau of Labor Statistics.

table 8.2) cut the increase in average hourly labor compensation back to 2.8 percent (6.1 minus 3.3), the same rate of growth as for labor productivity.

Table 8.2. Productivity and Costs: U.S. Private Business Sector, 1948–76
(percentage change from previous year)

Year	Output per All Person Hour	Compensation per Hour	Unit Labor Cost	Implicit Price Deflator	Real Compensation per Hour[a]	Real Compensation per Hour[b]
1948	3.9	8.6	4.5	8.4	1.0	0.2
1949	1.7	1.8	0.1	−1.1	2.6	3.0
1950	8.0	7.1	−0.8	1.5	6.1	5.8
1951	2.9	9.8	6.7	7.3	1.7	2.0
1952	2.5	6.4	3.8	1.9	3.9	4.7
1953	3.7	6.6	2.9	0.6	5.9	5.9
1954	1.8	3.4	1.5	0.9	2.9	2.4
1955	4.1	2.6	−1.5	1.5	3.0	1.0
1956	1.4	6.7	5.2	3.0	5.1	3.6
1957	3.0	6.7	3.7	3.2	3.2	3.4
1958	2.7	4.7	1.9	1.9	1.7	2.8
1959	3.6	4.6	1.0	2.0	3.6	2.6
1960	1.6	4.2	2.6	1.4	2.8	2.8
1961	3.3	4.0	0.7	0.6	3.1	3.3
1962	4.6	4.7	0.1	0.9	3.3	3.9
1963	4.0	3.9	−0.1	0.9	2.8	2.9
1964	4.1	5.4	1.3	1.4	3.9	4.0
1965	3.7	3.9	0.2	1.6	2.3	2.2
1966	3.2	7.0	3.7	3.2	4.0	3.8
1967	2.3	5.6	3.3	2.9	2.8	2.7
1968	3.3	7.6	4.1	3.9	3.2	3.6
1969	0.3	7.0	6.6	4.7	1.4	2.1
1970	0.7	7.2	6.4	4.7	1.3	2.4
1971	3.2	6.6	3.2	4.4	2.1	2.1
1972	2.9	5.7	2.7	3.6	2.4	1.9
1973	1.9	8.2	6.2	5.8	1.8	2.3
1974	−3.4	9.3	13.2	10.3	−1.5	−0.9
1975	2.1	9.7	7.5	9.5	0.5	0.1
1976	4.5	8.2	3.6	4.6	2.3	3.6
Avg. annual rate, 1947 –76	2.8	6.1	3.2	3.3	2.7	2.8

a. Compensation deflated by Consumer Price Index.
b. Compensation delfated by the implicit price deflator for private business sector.

SOURCE: Department of Labor, Bureau of Labor Statistics.

Cyclical Relationships

A basic problem of a guidepost approach, in addition to the difficulties of applying averages, is that a free economy does not move smoothly up a growth trend. It fluctuates both absolutely and in rates of change. Fluctuations in rates of change in productivity, average earnings, unit costs, prices, and profit rates are an integral part of business cycles. Indeed, as long ago as 1913 Wesley C. Mitchell recognized the interrelated movements of these variables as a major part of the explanation of cycles.[2] Subsequent research, using the much better statistics available in recent years, has confirmed Mitchell's theory and demonstrated that it explains cycles since World War II, as well as before, though with a few variations.[3]

The following exposition explains the interrelated movements of the variables over a typical U.S. postwar business cycle. It should first be noted that the average peacetime cycle since 1945 has lasted forty-five months—thirty-four months of expansion between the lower and upper turning points and eleven months of contraction back down to a lower turning point.[4] In addition to describing the typical cycle, we shall refer to the recent cycle that peaked in the fourth quarter of 1973 and reached its low in the first quarter of 1975.

We begin the explanation in the latter phase of expansion, when productivity advance begins to slow down and wage-rate increases speed up. This accelerates the rise in unit labor costs, which eventually presses against prices and squeeze profit margins, thereby turning the economy down as business outlays are reduced.

Productivity increase slows in late expansion because, as the expansion proceeds, production is pushed up to and beyond the most efficient rate of utilization of capacity in an increasing number of industries. Selective shortages of supply develop, and the time between the placement of orders and delivery lengthens. Less efficient stand-by plants are pressed into service. Even the new plants that come onstream, reflecting increased investment earlier in the expansion, require some time to "shake down" and reach full operating efficiency.

As employment expands and the normal frictional rate of un-employment is approached, less efficient workers are employed, including those who had been unemployed for extended periods of time. Further, the existence of relatively full employment and the ease of securing jobs tend to increase labor turnover and weaken work discipline to some extent. The number of strikes to secure higher pay increases and other benefits tends to rise. With profit margins at relatively high levels during a boom, management becomes less cost-conscious and may permit un-necessary waste and inefficiency to develop. Some manage-ments become less resistant to rising labor demands, expecting to recapture increased unit labor costs through price hikes.

The applicability of this generalized description to 1973 is ap-parent. After a smart expansion from 1971 thorugh the first quarter of 1973, productivity gains tapered as the capacity of most basic industries was reached. Shortages developed in steel and aluminum products, paper products, electric power, and pe-troleum refining, among others. Delays in deliveries were wide-spread. It was the oil embargo imposed in October 1973, of course, that led to the overall production drop by the end of the year, which began the first phase of the recent contraction.

What are the economic consequences of the decelerating rate of productivity advance? Typically, in conjunction with an in-crease in wage-rate boosts, the decelerating productivity trend results in accelerated increases in unit labor costs. Average hourly labor compensation accelerates because of reduced un-employment and tight labor markets. Not only are unions in a good bargaining position to demand and obtain higher increases in earnings, but competition among employers for labor also drives wages of nonunion workers up faster. At some point, labor costs per unit begin rising faster than prices, as macro-economic policy seeks to restrain the accelerating inflation. At this point, a squeeze on profit margins begins to develop, which eventually leads to a reduction in new investment commitments and a lower rate of inventory accumulation and thereby to a general economic contraction. This is not the invariable se-quence, of course, since each cycle has unique features. But profit margins and the ratio of prices to unit labor costs are among the more reliable leading indicators of cyclical turning points, as identified by the National Bureau of Economic Research.

The classical pattern emerged in 1973. Unit labor cost increases accelerated, reflecting both a faster increase of average hourly earnings and a slower growth of productivity, particularly the latter. By the second quarter, unit labor cost increases were outpacing prices. There was also a leveling out of corporate profits, as mentioned above, and a mild decline in profit margins as percentages of sales or assets.

Actually, the contraction in overall production between the fourth quarter of 1973 and early 1974 was not the classical type of downturn. It was due chiefly to the drop in petroleum supplies; aggregate demand held up quite well through the summer, and weakness was confined to a few areas, notably new residential construction and automobile sales. It was only by the last quarter of 1974 that the net change in real aggregate demand moved decisively downward. The continued acceleration in unit labor costs and erosion of profit margins played a role in the commencement of this second stage of contraction, which was marked by a sharp rise in the unemployment rate from an average 5.5 percent in the third quarter of 1974 to over 8 percent in early 1975.

After the peak of the business cycle, productivity advance usually continues to decelerate, or even declines, for two or three quarters into the recession (which averaged four quarters before the current contraction). But typically, one or two quarters before the trough, productivity growth quickens again (see table 8.3). The one exception was in the short and shallow three-quarter contraction of 1960–61, when productivity did not rise until general economic activity began to expand.

Why does productivity growth fall after the cycle peak but pick up before the trough? In the first place, in the early months of a recession businessmen are not certain that the contraction is real, and they delay laying off workers, hoping to avoid the costs of labor turnover and the risk of being unable to hire comparable workers later. In 1974 employment actually continued to rise through September despite the lowered production in the private economy. As the decline in production

Table 8.3. Percentage Changes in Output per Hour[a]
(1973–74 compared with average cycle)

1973–74		Average Cycle	
Quarter	Percentage Change	Quarter	Percentage Change
1973			
I	4.7	P-3	1.5
II	3.1	P-2	1.8
III	1.5	P-1	1.5
IV(P)	0.4	P	0.9
1974			
I	–2.1	P+1	1.2
II	–2.4	P+2	0.6
III	–2.9	P+3	1.3
IV	–3.6	P+4	2.5

[a] Percentage changes are computed from same quarter in previous year.

Table refers to U.S. Private nonfarm economy 1973–74 by quarters and to average experience in four previous cycles before and after peak quarter (P).

SOURCE: Bureau of Labor Statistics, U.S. Department of Labor.

accelerated in the fourth quarter, it became apparent that the contraction was serious. Employment and hours were cut back, though not as fast as production, and productivity suffered its most severe drop of the year.

Productivity also declines because production in an increasing number of industries falls below the most efficient rates of utilization of capacity, and average real costs per unit rise. Through the first three quarters of 1974 this situation was combined, curiously, with continued uneconomically high rates of utilization in some basic industries whose materials output continued in short supply.

In the latter phase of contraction, however, productivity generally begins to rise under the pressures on management of declining profits and on labor of rising unemployment. As managements become increasingly cost-conscious, they close less efficient plants, lay off less efficient workers as seniority rules may permit, and generally seek to tighten up efficiency. As employees place more value on their jobs, voluntary turnover drops and labor efficiency rises. Before the trough, also, the rate of decline in output is decelerating, so that the lessened negative impact of declining rates of capacity utilization can be more readily offset by the positive, productivity-enhancing measures. Before the trough of production, as noted earlier, hours are being cut faster than output, so that productivty typically starts upward before aggregate demand and production.

Up through the 1960–61 contraction the rate of increase of average hourly labor compensation began falling with the first quarter of recession. Consequently, unit labor costs decelerated promptly when productivity advance began rising. By the third quarter of the recession, unit labor costs were rising less rapidly than prices, helping to widen profit margins and set the stage for recovery. In the 1969–70 contraction, however, wage-rates increases continued to rise for three quarters before declining in the trough quarter. The acceleration of productivity a quarter before the trough caused the rise of unit labor costs to decelerate, and by the trough quarter the rise of unit labor costs was less than that of prices. So even in 1970 profit margins widened before recovery, but with less of a lead than in most previous cycles.

Once recovery sets in, productivity rises smartly for at least the first year—averaging about 4.5 percent, well above the trend-rate (see table 8.4). Much of the above-average rate of advance is due to the rising utilization of capacity toward the most efficient rates, which reverses the negative influence of falling utilization rates during the contraction. Labor turnover remains low, and the quality of workers available for new hires is higher than during the boom. Materials shortages are rare.

Table 8.4. Percentage Changes in Output per Hour
(1975–76 compared with average recovery)

Quarter	Percentage Change	
	1975–76 Recovery[b]	Average Cycle
T+1	1.5	2.8
T+2	4.6	4.1
T+3	5.0	5.0
T+4	6.2	5.5

SOURCE: Bureau of Labor Statistics, U.S. Department of Labor.

a. Average cycle: U.S. private nonfarm economy averages during past four quarters following cycle trough (T); 1975–76 recovery: second quarter 1975 through first quarter 1976.

Average hourly labor compensation also begins rising more rapidly during the first year out from the trough. But since much of this rise is offset by higher productivity gains, unit labor costs increase slowly—or they may even continue downward, as they did in 1961. Unit labor costs in early expansion have risen uniformly less than prices, however, presumably because of expansionary monetary policies. Thus profit margins widen, helping to fuel the expansion. This was notably the case from 1975 to 1976, when unit labor costs rose 3.5 percent while prices increased by 5 percent.

During the second year of expansion, and sometimes longer, prices continue to rise as much as or more than unit labor costs, forestalling any prolonged profit squeeze. But once production reaches or exceeds the most efficient rates of utilization of capacity in a number of basic industries and unemployment gets down to the normal frictional range, the tendency for unit labor costs to accelerate strengthens. This eventually results in the profit squeeze with which we began the explanation.

Although the productivity-cost-price relation is a central part of the explanation of cycles, it is not the whole story, of course. The actions of the monetary authorities—limiting the increase of the money supply and prices in boom periods but easing financial conditions in recession—are important. So is the fiscal policy of the federal government, which tends to result in surpluses during booms and deficits during recessions. Also, the behavior of investment, particularly the swings in inventory accumulation, must be taken into account. But our purpose here was to explain the role of productivity in cycles.

Achievement of a steadier rate of economic growth would tend to result in a somewhat stronger trend-rate of productivity advance. This is true because of the reduction in capital outlays during contractions, including those that are cost-saving and productivity-enhancing. Also, during prolonged periods of unemployment there is some erosion of labor skills and there are income losses, which reduce the human investments that are essential to increasing productivity. It remains a challenge to economists to devise policy measures for avoiding the distortions that develop during booms, in order to achieve steadier and stronger growth.

9

Prospects for the Decade Ahead

Knowledge of past trends and relationships, causal factors, and economic impacts—which we have covered in the preceding chapters—is a prerequisite for projecting productivity and associated variables into the future. Long-range projections, for a decade or so ahead, are helpful for governments and private organizations that are trying to formulate broad policies and strategies for influencing and adapting to basic trends. Projections and plans have to be modified periodically, of course, to take account of subsequent developments, since forecasting is still more an art than a science. Nevertheless, governments and most larger private organizations find it useful to engage in such exercises.

In this chapter, we first speculate about the probable national productivity trend over the next decade. Then we present some projections developed by the Department of Labor on an industry basis.

Prospective Trends in the U.S. Private Economy[1]

In looking ahead, it is important to realize the strength and persistence of an upward productivity trend in the U.S. private economy. On a total factor basis, it has averaged about 2.2

percent a year for about sixty years. One reason for the relatively good record of long-term projections of real GNP has been the reasonably steady growth of productivity. It is true that there have been periods of acceleration and deceleration in productivity advance, as is true of most economic time-series. Notably, there was the marked slowdown of the latter 1960s, which led some to fear a permanent deceleration. But most of the depressing factors appear to have been temporary—with the possible exception of the reduced growth of the research and development stock, and even that was due mainly to the cutback of publicly financed and largely defense- and space-related activity. Certainly, the virtual recovery of the productivity rate in the 1969–73 period puts the burden of proof on those who expect the deceleration to continue.

The present writer's appraisal is that the rate of productivity advance is more likely than not to accelerate over the next decade compared with the past decade, particularly in terms of output per hour. This view is based on more than mechanical extrapolation of the long swing, in which periods of slow growth in real product and productivity are invariably followed by periods of above-average advance. It is based in part on the deeper view that there are "cybernetic" forces in the economy and in the broader society that lead to the correction of unfavorable tendencies—either through built-in stabilizers or as a result of conscious policies to reverse the negative trends once they are recognized as such.

In this chapter, the analytical framework developed earlier is used to evaluate qualitatively the direction of the effect of the significant variables on the rate of productivity advance relative to the trend rate since 1946 and relative to the somewhat lower rate of the past decade (see table 4.1, ch. 4). It would be more elegant if we could construct a model with precise coefficients to indicate the productivity impacts of projected changes in the significant independent variables. But the productivity variable is so complex, reflecting the net effect of myriad economic, social, and natural phenomena, that no credible econometric model has yet been constructed. Even if it could be, the projections of the independent variables would be far more crucial than the system of equations embodied in the model. And, of course, the coefficients based on past relationships might well change over a forecast period of as long as a decade. The effort here is more modest—to bring judgment to bear on the probable course of the major causal factors relative to past trends (summarized in table 9.1) and then attempt to weigh the net impact.

Table 9.1. Factors Affecting Productivity Growth: Qualitative Appraisal of Expected Influence, 1976–86

	Decade 1976–86 relative to period:	
	1946–66	*1966–76*
Basic determinants		
Values and attitudes	0	+
Institutional forms and practices	0	+
Proximate determinants		
Short-run		
Capacity utilization rates	0	+
Labor efficiency/standars	0	+
Long-run		
Tangible investments	0	−
Intangible investments		
Research and development	−	0
Education and training	0	0
Health, safety, etc.	+	0
Economies of scale	0	+
Natural resources quality	−	−
Economic efficiency	0	+

0 = neutral relative to influence in earlier period;
+ = positive influence; − = negative influence.

Looking first at the underlying forces, I believe that basic values and attitudes still favor economic progress in the United States. The so-called hippie culture never really took hold of significant population groups, and even hippies engaged in productive activity, sometimes outside the market system. Americans still appear to desire increasing real income for themselves and their children, judging from their actions as individuals and as members of such organizations as trade unions. True, as average education rises, people are more concerned with the quality of work and of working life; but if increased job satisfaction is realized, it should promote productivity. Further, the efforts of women and various minority groups to attain income parity should also increase incentives for higher productivity. The ending of the involvement in Vietnam in 1973 reduced the appeal of various radical groups and increased the willingness of social critics to work within the system to achieve desirable social change.

Although criticism of the business economy undoubtedly mounted during the past decade, there does not appear to be widespread sentiment to alter radically our predominantly private-enterprise, market-directed economy, with its rewards for superior performance and penalties for inefficiency. The reports of many of the foreign productivity teams that visited the United States after World War II emphasized the view that our competitive market system was "the secret of American prosperity." Some of the socialist systems are experimenting with greater reliance on the price mechanism as a means of spurring managers to devise and adopt cost-reducing innovations. In our own system, in the regulated sector there is a trend toward reducing the number of regulated areas, and elsewhere to develop regulatory techniques that encourage and reward superior productivity performance. Even in the areas in which governmental intervention has increased, such as environmental protection and occupational safety, there is pressure to develop more reasonable standards with an eye to the cost-benefit relations and trade-offs with other objectives, such as productivity advance and energy conservation and development.

One small but significant institutional innovation was the creation in July 1970 of what is now called the National Center for Productivity and Quality of Working Life. This was a response to the productivity slowdown of the latter 1960s, and it illustrates the "cybernetic" mechanism referred to earlier. In addition to encouraging productivity measurement, analysis, and promotion in the private and public sectors, the National Center is in a position to assess the productivity impacts of existing and proposed governmental programs and thus aid in developing policies to accelerate productivity advance.

On balance, it is my impression that the basic forces in the economy that condition productivity growth—human values and

93

the legal and institutional framework of the economy—are more favorable in 1977 than those prevailing during the productivity slowdown after 1966 and comparable to those of the proceeding two decades of relatively strong productivity advance, 1946 to 1966. They may even become more favorable, but such a prediction would be very speculative.

Of the proximate determinants of productivity increase, several appear to be more favorable for the next decade than for the last. One is a predominantly short-run factor, rates of utilization of capacity. In the last quarter of 1975, the Commerce Department estimate of the manufacturing capacity utilization rate was 79, compared with 85 for 1969 and 86 for 1973. The Federal Reserve Board series showed 71, compared with 86.5 for 1969 and 83 for 1973. So, if relatively full employment is assumed for 1985–86, it is clear that the decadal productivity growth rate from the 1975–76 level will receive a boost from the movement toward more efficient rates of utilization of capacity. Likewise, opportunities for economies of scale will be greater from 1975–76 to 1985–86—although the basic growth trend of real GNP, projected by the BLS at 3.6 percent for the 1973–85 period, will be the same as from 1966 to 1973 and a bit below the 1948–66 rate of about 4.0 percent per annum.

If I am right that values and attitudes have improved since the end of the Vietnam conflict, then labor efficiency may well be higher relative to norms in the decade ahead than in the 1966–73 period and more in line with performance in the preceding two decades. Unfortunately, aggregate measures are not available in this area. Also, possible improvements in worker health and safety resulting from OSHA and EPA requirements and accelerated investments in these areas, should tend to raise productivity in coming years.

We come now to the factors associated with the rate of capital formation. The National Science Foundation projects that the ratio of research and development to GNP will stabilize at about 2 percent for the next decade. This means that the stock of intangible capital resulting from research and development will increase at a rate similar to that of recent years but at a lower rate than during the previous decades, when research and development was rising in relation to GNP. The possible impact on productivity advance will be mitigated by two factors: first, the decline in R&D outlays was concentrated in federally funded, defense- and space-related activities, which have relatively little impact on productivity; and second, with a slower growth of R&D outlays relative to the period before 1966, the projects undertaken may well have a higher-than-average rate of return and productivity effect. Nevertheless, the lower R&D/GNP ratio is not a favorable factor.

Education and training outlays and the growth of embodied intangible capital per worker are expected to increase during the next decade at the rates experienced in the past several decades, according to projections by the Department of Health, Education and Welfare. Also, the relative shift of students away from science, engineering, and business administration in the late 1960s and early 1970s appears to have been reversed. As noted earlier, the growth of intangible stocks per worker resulting from health and safety outlays was one variable that accelerated in the 1966–76 period relative to earlier years, partly because of OSHA requirements. It is expected that the growth will continue above the earlier rates in the coming decade.

Tangible capital formation, of particular importance as a carrier of technological progress, has proceeded at a fairly steady trend-rate ever since World War II. It has been slow in recovering from the 1973–75 contraction. But if after-tax rates of return are restored to a "normal" range, the rate of increase in the real stocks should approximate past trends. As noted earlier, the significant increase in the proportion of real investment devoted to antipollution, occupational health and safety, and energy conservation purposes contributed to the productivity slowdown; the outputs of these programs are not included in the productivity measures, but the inputs are. But as the proportions of new investments devoted to these purposes level out and possibly declne over the next decade, the negative effect will be removed. Also, as the required investments shift from a "patch-up" basis to a basis in which they are designed for integration with new plants and equipment, positive productivity results will emerge.[2]

We come now to noninvestment forces. Economies of scale were discussed earlier. With regard to economic (allocative) efficiency, there has been little change in the degrees of concentration and unionization of American industry; nor does much change seem likely in the next decade. The degree of government intervention did increase, beginning in the 1930s and culminating in the 1971–74 wage and price controls, which resulted in relative price distortions with effects on resource allocation. The elimination of direct controls and the tendency toward less government intervention should result in greater economic efficiency in the decade ahead than in the past decade. But otherwise it seems unlikely that there will be much change in the efficiency of the market pricing mechanism as a means of allocating resources.

Connected with allocation is the effect of changing product mix by industry on productivity. With respect to total factor productivity, the chief effect of changing mix relates to the weights assigned to differential industry rates of productivity change. Outside of farming and the service industries, there is a tendency for output to rise more in industries in which productivity is rising at above-average rates and relative unit costs and prices are falling. But in agriculture, low income elasticity of demand and above-average productivity advance have caused resources to flow out; in services, high income elasticity and below-average productivity advance have caused resources to flow in. These tendencies have dampened national productivity advance. The trends are expected to continue. But if the relative shift out of extractive industry and into services is no faster than in the past, it will have no net effect on productivity advance. The BLS projections suggest that the shift may accelerate slightly in the next decade, but the acceleration is so minor and so uncertain that we would predict no significant effect on the productivity trend.

The average quality of natural resources is undoubtedly declining, and so there is a consequent tendency toward diminishing returns. Until recent years this tendency was more than offset by technological advance. But since 1966, the rate of increase of productivity in mineral industries has decelerated. It also appears that the rate may have decelerated mildly in agriculture since 1969. If the programs designed to achieve greater relative energy independence in the decade ahead go forward, there may be an even greater negative impact on productivity than would be the case if imports of fuels were admitted freely. But the total effect should be relatively small, in view of the modest share of total costs accounted for by raw materials in general and energy materials in particular.

On balance, I would expect the rate of increase of total factor productivity in the U.S. economy as a whole in the decade from 1976 to 1986 to be somewhat above the 1.7 percent rate of the 1966–73 period. In part, this would reflect a move from cyclically depressed rates of utilization of capacity to more efficient rates, assuming 1986 is a year of relatively high, or even average, activity. More fundamentally, this prediction reflects the lifting of some of the negative forces affecting productivity in recent years, particularly during the 1966–70 period, as reviewed above.

Abstracting from cyclical forces, however, I would expect that the trend-rate of total factor productivity advance in the next decade would be modestly below the 2.4 percent rate of the 1948–66 period. Basically, this would reflect a slightly slower growth rate of R&D; slower productivity advances in extractive industries, and particularly in production of energy materials; and fewer opportunities for economies of scale as economic growth generally slows down somewhat with a deceleration in the growth of the labor force in the 1980s. There will be some offset to these negative factors as the proportion of investments and costs devoted to antipollution, health and safety, and energy conservation programs stabilizes or possibly declines and as a productivity payoff from these programs emerges.

The rate of increase in output per hour in the decade ahead may well equal the longer-run trend-rate of somewhat better than 3 percent a year, on average. This more optimistic assessment of prospects for labor productivity relative to total factor productivity is based on the expected retardation of labor force growth. The U.S. Department of Labor projects a 1.2 average annual rate from 1980 to 1985, compared with about 2.0 percent from 1966 to 1973. Assuming that savings and investment propensities are maintained at their past levels, this means that capital per worker will grow significantly faster in the latter part of the decade ahead, than in the first part. Since the rate of increase in output per hour is positively correlated with real capital per hour, the growth of labor productivity should accelerate relative to the growth of total factor productivity. Thus, real income per worker may be expected to grow in line with past secular trends, assuming that average number of hours worked per year does not drop faster in the future than it has in the past.

The foregoing review of the various forces that will affect productivity in the years ahead makes plain the enormous complexity of the problem, the difficulties of projection, and the large margins of error that must surround a projection. The saving graces are the tendency for errors in the projections of individual factors to offset each other and the persistence of underlying trends in aggregates.

It must be noted that the discussion of productivity prospects has been predicated on the continuation of present and prospective institutional forms, practices, and policies short of the adoption of major programs designed to accelerate productivity advance. Such new programs certainly are not out of the question, in view of the wide publicity given to the productivity slowdown and mounting public and official concern. In chapter 10, we present an overview of the sorts of policies that could result in the American economy's resuming a productivity growth rate equal to that of the 1946–66 period, or possibly somewhat above it, in the decade ahead.

It is reassuring that essentially the same conclusions regarding the intermediate-term productivity outlook were reached by Edward F. Denison of the Brookings Institution and Jerome Mark of the Bureau of Labor Statistics in papers presented at a 1977 symposium sponsored by the National Center.[3] Mark's analysis is reflected in BLS projections of a 2.4 percent average annual rate of increase of productivity in the U.S. private economy from 1973 to 1980 and 2.7 percent from 1980 to 1985. The smaller rate for the 1973–80 period takes account of the cyclical decline of productivity in 1974–75. But even the 2.7 percent rate, though above the 1966–73 rate, is below the 1948–66 trend.

The productivity projection is, of course, necessary to translate projections of labor force, employment, and hours worked into real GNP projections. The BLS projects real GNP growth at a 3.8 average annual rate between 1972 and 1985—close to the previous growth rate. The growth rate is expected to decelerate only slightly after 1980, despite a marked slowdown in the growth of labor force and hours worked due to the acceleration in growth of output per hour, as noted above.

Another way to state it is that a 3.8 percent yearly average growth of real GNP is necessary, given the productivity projection, in order to absorb the projected growth in the labor force of 13.7 million persons between 1976 and 1985 and to reduce the unemployment rate to 4 percent of the civilian labor force, if that is the goal.

Productivity Projections by Industry

For a number of purposes, it is useful to project productivity on an industry basis. This is basic to projecting relative price changes over intermediate-term or longer-run periods, as explained in chapter 5. The relative price movements, in turn, help in projecting relative sales and output, by industry. Given the industry output (or real product) projections, the projections for output per worker (or per hour) can then be applied to obtain the future industrial composition of employment.

Essentially this approach was used by the BLS in its projections for 1985,[4] except that to obtain output projections real GNP was broken down into product categories, which were allocated by industry. Then, by use of an input-output table based on interindustry sales and purchases, total sales and production of each industry were obtained (see table 9.2).

To project productivity by industry, ideally one should try to project all the significant causal variables, as discussed in chapters 5 and 7—rate of output growth, cyclical variability of output, R&D outlays, rate of tangible investment, average education of workers, and other characteristics of the labor force, such as degree of unionization. But some of these variables on an industry basis would be subject to wide margins of error, and the BLS used a rather simpler procedure. It

Table 9.2. Real Product in the U.S. Private Economy (in billions of 1963 dollars)

	1973	1980	1985	Average Annual Percentage Change	
				1973-80	1980-85
Total Private Economy	$820.4	$1,064.0	$1,273.1	3.8%	3.7%
Agriculture	24.4	28.6	30.8	2.3	1.5
Nonagriculture	796.0	1,035.4	1,242.3	3.8	3.1
Mining	13.6	14.2	17.2	0.6	3.9
Construction	41.9	47.7	56.7	1.9	3.5
Manufacturing	280.5	350.3	416.7	3.2	3.5
Durable	156.1	198.3	235.8	3.5	3.5
Nondurable	124.4	152.0	180.9	2.9	3.5
Transportation, Communications, and Public Utilities	90.5	127.5	161.1	5.0	4.8
Transportation	37.7	51.9	62.7	4.7	3.9
Communications	29.0	41.5	55.0	5.3	5.8
Public Utilities	23.8	34.1	43.4	5.3	4.9
Trade	142.7	191.7	222.2	4.3	3.0
Wholesale	56.3	77.0	89.1	4.6	3.0
Retail	86.4	114.7	133.1	4.1	3.0
Finance, Insurance, and Real Estate	117.8	157.2	191.2	4.2	4.0
Other Services	96.3	129.1	156.5	4.3	3.9
Government Enterprises	13.8	18.8	22.6	4.5	3.8
(Statistical Discrepancies)	(-1.1)	(-1.1)	(-1.1)	—	—

SOURCE: Bureau of Labor Statistics, U.S. Department of Labor.

extrapolated recent trends, modified by the projected changes in output growth, the growth in real capital investment per worker, and any known technological developments of importance to the industry.

Table 9.3 summarizes the results by broad industry groups. Note that productivity growth in finance is expected to accelerate to a 2.1 percent average annual rate in the 1980–85 period from 1.4 percent between 1968 and 1980, in view of the expected spread of electronic data processing, transfer, and other equipment. On the other hand, productivity in communications is expected to increase at an average 4.3 percent annual rate through 1985, up from the earlier period. Agriculture is expected to experience average productivity gains of about 6 percent annually in both periods because of continued increases in mechanization, use of fertilizers and other chemicals, and other technologies that have contributed to the above-average gains of the past forty years.

The distribution of productivity gains by rate-of-change classes will be as much as in the past. Of the 112 more detailed industries for which the BLS prepared projections, 30 are expected to register productivity gains of more than 4 percent a year, and 31 to show increases of less than 2 percent. The remaining 51 industries are projected to achieve productivity gains of 2 to 4 percent a year, on average.

By subtracting the projected rates of productivity change (making allowance for changes in average hours worked) from the rates of change in output, the projected rates of change of employment were derived. These are shown in table 9.4, together with absolute employment levels for 1973, 1980, and 1985, for major industry groups. The total number of civilian jobs is projected to increase at a 1.8 percent average annual rate from 1973 to 1980, then at 1.5 percent annually between 1980 and 1985, reflecting the retardation in growth of the labor force. Although federal government civilian employment is expected to increase at about half the rate of the total (and armed forces to hold constant at about 2.0 million), state and local government employment is projected to grow at about double the private economy rate. The number of persons engaged in agriculture will continue to decline. In the private nonfarm econ-

Table 9.3. Real Product per Hour in the U.S. Private Economy (in 1963 dollars)

	1973	1980	1985	Average Annual Percentage Change	
				1973–80	1980–85
Total Private Economy	$ 5.51	$ 6.51	$ 7.45	2.4%	2.7%
Agriculture	3.17	4.77	6.30	6.0	5.7
Nonagriculture	5.64	6.58	7.48	2.2	2.6
Mining	10.37	9.43	11.06	-1.3	3.2
Construction	4.47	4.82	5.18	1.1	1.5
Manufacturing	7.04	8.36	9.76	2.5	3.1
Durable	6.65	7.89	9.14	2.5	3.0
Nondurable	7.61	9.05	10.72	2.5	3.4
Transportation, Communications, and Public Utilities	9.54	12.87	15.85	4.4	4.3
Transportation	6.56	8.91	10.77	4.5	3.9
Communications	12.66	16.60	20.46	3.9	4.3
Public Utilities	16.48	21.52	26.20	3.9	4.0
Trade	3.77	4.47	5.07	2.5	2.6
Wholesale	6.54	8.01	9.23	2.9	2.9
Retail	2.96	3.44	3.90	2.2	2.5
Finance, Insurance, and Real Estate	13.63	15.26	16.97	1.6	2.1
Other Services	2.78	3.16	3.43	1.8	1.7
Government Enterprises	4.92	5.82	6.67	2.4	2.8

SOURCE: Bureau of Labor Statistics, U.S. Department of Labor

Table 9.4. U.S. Total Employment: Jobs Count by Major Sector (in thousands)

	1973	1980	1985	Annual Percentage Change 1973–80	Annual Percentage Change 1980–85
Total	89,654	101,866	109,565	1.8	1.5
Government	13,739	16,800	19,350	2.9	2.9
Federal	2,663	2,900	3,000	1.2	0.7
State and local	11,075	13,900	16,350	3.3	3.3
Private	75,915	85,066	90,215	1.6	1.2
Farm	5,423	2,750	2,300	-2.6	-3.1
Nonfarm	72,492	82,316	87,915	1.8	1.3
Mining	674	788	823	2.3	0.9
Construction	4,821	5,178	5,798	1.0	0.6
Manufacturing	20,468	21,937	22,597	1.0	0.6
Durable	12,067	13,148	13,661	1.2	0.8
Nondurable	8,401	8,789	8,936	0.3	0.3
Transportation, Communications, and Public Utilities	4,874	5,186	5,381	0.9	0.7
Transportation	2,955	3,049	3,081	0.4	0.2
Communications	1,177	1,308	1,423	1.5	1.7
Public Utilities	742	829	877	1.6	1.1
Trade	19,432	22,457	23,187	2.1	0.6
Wholesale	4,424	5,029	5,109	1.8	0.3
Retail	15,008	17,428	18,078	2.2	0.7
Finance, Insurance, and Real Estate	4,442	5,392	5,964	2.8	2.0
Other Services	17,781	21,378	24,165	2.7	2.5
Government Enterprises	1,441	1,690	1,795	2.3	1.2

SOURCE: Bureau of Labor Statistics, U.S. Department of Labor.
NOTE: Detail may not add to totals because of rounding.

omy, the dispersion of rates of growth is not particularly wide. The lowest rates of employment growth are expected in nondurable goods manufacturing and in transportation, both at less than 0.5 percent a year. The highest rates of growth are projected for finance and services, reflecting the relatively low rates of productivity increase. Most of the industries are expected to show some deceleration in employment growth after 1980; the contract construction and communications industries are exceptions.

When the projections are spelled out in greater industry detail, the dispersion of rates of employment growth increases. Thus, the top tenth of industries is expected to increase employment by 4.5 percent in the 1973–80 period and by 3.5 percent between 1980 and 1985. Examples of fast-growth industries are finance, medical services, and miscellaneous professional services. The lowest tenth will show employment declines averaging 2.2 percent between 1973 and 1980 and 1.9 percent from 1980 to 1985. This group includes railroads, livestock products, tobacco manufacturing, and mining of nonmetallic minerals. Among industries with employment growth close to the private economy average are trucking, paper and allied products, and chemicals.

Using statistics on the occupational composition of employment in various industries, the BLS is also able to project employment by occupational categories. Though carried out in terms of about 400 categories, these have been consolidated into 37 occupational groupings. The largest increases are expected in employment of health service workers, at about 5.0 percent a year between 1974 and 1985. Computer technicians, stenographers, and clerical workers in general are also expected to experience large increases in employment demand. The numbers of teachers and of workers in the printing trades are expected to show low growth, and declining employment is likely for farm occupations, private household work, and semi-skilled textile jobs. In general, the projections show higher growth rates in professional and skilled occupations and lower growth rates in semi-skilled occupations.

The projections make it clear that there will continue to be substantial changes in the industrial and occupational composition of the employed labor force in coming years, as in the past. These shifts reflect both continuing technological changes, which have differential impacts on various industries, and the other dynamic forces affecting supply and demand. The projected changes in patterns of output, productivity, and employment underscore the need to make further improvements in national and organizational policies to facilitate labor mobility as well as to promote productivity. It is to this area we turn in the final chapters.

10

Public Policies
to Promote and Accommodate Productivity Advance

Up to this point we have assumed that economic progress (defined as increases in real product per capita) is desirable. In this chapter we begin with a critical discussion of the goal of economic progress and indicate certain qualifications that attach to that goal. But we conclude that, whatever the material objective, rationality requires continued productivity advance as a major means of achieving that goal. Next we review the role of public policy in promoting productivity. Then we enumerate the main undesirable by-products of the technological progress that underlies productivity advance and consider the policy measures required to obviate them.

The Goal of Economic Progress

After World War II virtually all nations embraced the goal of economic progress. Many of the richer nations, individually and through the United Nations, have adopted programs for helping the less developed countries increase their output and income per capita. The more advanced countries, including the United States, also have the national goal of increasing output and income per capita in order to meet the rising levels of material aspirations of their citizens.

In recent years, increasing numbers of people have begun to question the desirability of continuing economic growth and progress, particularly in the United States and the advanced countries of Western Europe. The critics have called attention to the undesirable fallouts of economic growth, in the forms of environmental pollution and the depletion of irreplaceable resources; they have pointed to the increasing social problems attendant on the urbanization and population congestion that accompany economic development; they have decried what they call the materialism of our civilization, pointing to the many other important aspects of individual and social welfare; and they have claimed that more attention should be paid to the distribution of income among various segments of the population than to the growth of income.

This critical attitude toward material progress has resulted in a more balanced view of the growth objective. It is becoming widely accepted that we must devote more of our resources and production to combating pollution and reversing deterioration of the physical environment. As in the past, shifts must be made from natural resources that are becoming scarce and relatively more expensive to those that are more abundant and relatively cheaper. Equally important, we must spend more of the national income for alleviating the undesirable broader social impacts of material progress and for helping the individuals and groups that bear the brunt of technological displacement of jobs and other costs of progress. As a corollary, society must improve its institutions and practices for preparing all people to take advantage of the opportunities afforded by economic progress and to share equitably in its fruits. Finally, the critics have helped remind us of what we have long known—that man does not live by bread alone and that material progress only provides the basis for progress in humanistic values, cultural activities, and the other facets of the good life.

Only a few of the extreme critics would advocate halting material progress altogether. Most countries of the world have not yet attained average incomes to meet what we would consider to be minimum standards of decency and comfort. Even in the United States, roughly one-eighth of the people live below such standards. But the most compelling argument in favor of continuing economic progress, with due allowance for improvements in the quality of the natural and social environments, is that people's aspirations continually outrun their attainments, and standards of living rise faster than attained planes of living. Most individuals in our society and most organized groups, such as labor unions, continue to strive to increase their real incomes and also gradually to increase the leisure time available in which to enjoy their incomes and to develop further their capacities and potentials for creative and satisfying work and other activities.

In the last analysis, it is not the intellectuals who debate about the optimum rate of economic growth who will determine it. Rather, the rate of growth will be the net outcome of the decisions of the many families of the country and of their organizations (including governments) concerning work and leisure, saving and consumption, and the mix of the various types of investment and consumer goods and services. Regardless of the rates of economic growth and progress that emerge from collective decisions, it is only rational to achieve them, in part at least, through an optimum rate of productivity advance. This implies continuation of the underlying scientific and technological progress—although an increasing proportion of our scientific resources will be devoted to mitigating undesirable by-products of economic growth, as well as to the traditional objectives of developing new and improved products and cost-reducing technologies.

The reason continued productivity advance is eminently rational is that the basic factors of production all have other desirable uses, so that economies in the consumption of labor, land, and capital per unit of output make possible an expansion of the alternative activities. In the case of labor, the alternative is leisure, and reduced hour requirements per unit of output will make possible a continuation of the trend toward shorter workweeks and workyears and thus the enjoyment of more cultural, recreational, and other leisure-time activities. In the case of natural resources, savings in consumption per unit of output make possible more conservation for future use, or greater use for recreational purposes in the case of certain types of resources. In the case of man-made capital, economies make greater consumption possible, since the alternative to the saving and investment required for capital formation is consumption expenditure.

Public Policies to Promote Productivity

In order to pursue appropriate policies to promote productivity, public officials and their advisers must understand the sources of productivity advance. Accordingly, this discussion of policy is organized around topics relating to the chief causes of productivity advance, as elaborated in chapter 7.

Values and Institutions

Values, of course, gradually change as conditions change and as a result of discussion and debate. But for the foreseeable future, we assume that Americans continue to value the objective of economic progress, for the reasons and with the qualifications noted above. Since productivity increase is the chief source of economic progress, public information programs of the National Center for Productivity and Quality of Working Life, and of other public and private agencies that seek to promote broader public understanding of basic economic principles, seem appropriate.

With regard to economic institutions, it seems likely that we shall continue, as in the past, to rely primarily on private property, the profit motive, and competition in free markets to stimulate economic progress and productivity advance. Under this system, firms with above-average productivity are rewarded by higher profit rates; those with below-average productivity are penalized by low profit rates, or even losses; and the least efficient firms tend to be driven out of business. To achieve these results, there must be continued and vigorous enforcement of the Sherman Anti-Trust Act of 1890 and of subsequent legislation designed to promote competition and efficiency, as administered by the Anti-Trust Division of the Justice Department and by the Federal Trade Commission.

In the areas of "natural monopoly"—transportation and public utilities—in which it is inefficient to have more than one firm in a given market area, the rates charged are regulated by public commissions, a practice that permits a profit rate similar to what would obtain under competition. Improvements are needed here in order to provide greater incentives to regulated firms to increase productivity. For example, productivity "bogeys" could be set, achievement of which would enable firms to earn rates of return at the upper limit of an established range.

Despite our chief reliance on competitive free enterprise plus regulation, the role of government in the economy has grown as the economy has become more complex. In particular, the federal government assumed responsibility for promoting "maximum production, employment, and purchasing power" with the Employment Act of 1946. This act set up the Council of Economic Advisers to the President and the Joint Economic Committee of Congress to develop policy measures to ensure attainment of the objectives of the act. As a result we have had no major depression since before World War II, with the possible exception of the 1973–75 contraction. This relatively stable growth has promoted productivity advance, since it has meant larger amounts of saving and investment in new and more efficient plants and equipment. Reasonably full employment must remain a major economic goal of the federal government, and even more effective measures must be devised to further stabilize growth rates.

The National Center for Productivity and Quality of Working Life, composed of both public and private members, is charged with the responsibility of making recommendations regarding measures required to promote productivity. The establishment of the National Center was a landmark in that no single permanent agency, including the Council of Economic Advisers, had previously focused attention on policies and programs to advance productivity and economic progress.

In October 1975, the National Commission on Productivity (predecessor to the National Center) issued its first major policy statement, "A National Policy for Productivity Improvement." It treated in a rather general way policy issues in the areas of human resources (labor-management relations, education and training, job security, and quality of working life), technology and capital investment, and government regulation. Reflecting its multipartite composition, the commission (and later the

National Center) apparently took a rather limited view of its policy role: "The Commission hopes that this expression of its views will serve to stimulate efforts by responsible individuals in all sectors of the economy to provide counsel to those charged with legislative and policy decision, and to improve the quality of the debate on issues for which solutions are still being sought."

It should be noted that in addition to providing support for the National Center, whose budget was less than $3 million in fiscal year 1976, the federal government spent $933 billion for activities in various agencies designed specifically to improve productivity. Some of this went to enhance human resources, to improve organization and management, and to measure and analyze productivity growth. But the bulk of it, $786 billion, was devoted to improving civilian technology. Table 10.1 shows the various activities and projects for which the obligations were incurred. It will be noted that the greatest portion went to improve agricultural and other natural resource technologies. The National Center, which collected the information about these programs, will assess their contributions to productivity growth and attempt to provide more effective coordination of the federal programs.

New Investments, Intangible and Tangible

The most important proximate determinant of increases in total tangible factor productivity is the intangible investment designed to improve the quality and efficiency of the tangible human and nonhuman factors of production. Such investments fall into four main categories, as discussed in chapter 7. The magnitude of the various types of intangible investment and their increases since 1929 are shown in table 10.2. There it can be seen that in the four decades after 1929, intangible investments increased in relation both to tangible investment and to GNP. This suggests that the amount of intangible capital embodied in the tangible human and nonhuman factors of production rose significantly over the period, and other estimates not shown here confirm this inference. It is clear, therefore, that the growth of intangible capital accounts for much of the increase in tangible factor productivity.

111

Table 10.1. Major Activities and Projects to Improve Civilian Technology in Industries, Services, Agriculture, and Government (obligations in millions of dollars)

Activity or Project	FY 1974	FY 1975	FY 1976
All activities and projects	426.9	588.8	786.3
Agricultural technology	*235.0*	*275.4*	*303.3*
Corp production efficiency	65.6	79.0	90.0
Animal production efficiency	35.4	42.4	48.6
Processing, storage, and distribution efficiency	35.9	47.6	50.3
Production and management programs	33.5	34.0	43.5
Cooperative state research service	60.6	68.3	75.3
Agriculture weather services	2.1	2.3	2.5
Research to expand agricultural exports	1.9	1.8	2.1
Forestry and timber technology	*44.8*	*54.7*	*57.3*
Timber management research	13.1	14.5	15.1
Forest disease, products, and engineering research	22.0	19.8	31.7
Forestry task force	1.9	2.2	2.1
Fire and atmospheric sciences research	7.8	8.2	8.4
Maritime transportation technology	*6.4*	*8.6*	*8.5*
Shipbuilding R&D	2.4	2.3	2.4
Ship machinery and automation R&D	1.2	2.3	2.5
Shipping operations information systems	1.3	2.0	0.9
Advanced ship R&D	–	0.7	0.9
Cargo handing R&D	–	0.4	0.3
Marine sciences R&D	1.4	0.8	1.4
Extending shipping season on Great Lakes	0.1	0.1	0.1
Fisheries technology	*7.8*	*10.2*	*12.1*
Fisheries development programs	0.4	0.8	2.4
Columbia River salmon program	4.3	6.0	5.9
Increasing use of fish resources	3.1	3.4	3.8
Manufacturing	*82.9*	*88.1*	*110.9*
Defense Department programs	77.0	80.0	91.0
Industry energy conservation	–	2.7	10.0
Private-sector productivity	4.1	3.2	6.8
Electronic technology measurement	1.1	1.2	1.7
Standard reference materials	0.5	0.4	0.6
Nondestructive evaluation program	–	0.4	0.6
Electromagnetic materials properties	0.2	0.2	0.2

(continued)

Table 10.1. (Continued)

Activity or Project	FY 1974	FY 1975	FY 1976
Mining technology	*19.6*	*61.0*	*76.1*
Advancing coal mining and preparation	6.8	43.3	55.5
Advancing metal and nonmetal mining technology	4.5	4.7	5.4
Advancing minerals technology	7.4	10.5	12.3
Mineral resources surveys and mapping	0.2	0.2	0.3
Surface environment and mining research	0.7	2.3	2.6
Electric power technology	–	*12.8*	*27.6*
High-voltage test facilities	–	4.0	4.0
Power-plant productivity improvement	–	0.3	0.4
Electrical energy systems R&D	–	6.2	13.7
Energy conservation	–	2.3	9.5
Energy technology	–	*28.5*	*112.6*
Solar energy application	–	13.1	68.8
Biomass fuels	–	0.1	3.8
Energy conservation	–	5.0	6.4
Transportation energy conservation	–	8.4	10.3
Coal demonstration	–	1.9	23.3
Construction technology	*0.4*	*6.2*	*22.5*
Research on rural housing construction	0.2	0.2	0.4
Energy standards and venting technology	0.2	0.2	0.1
Energy storage	–	5.8	13.8
Building energy conservation	–	–	8.2
Services	*7.1*	*9.1*	*9.1*
Postsecondary education	–	–	0.2
Computer-assisted instruction	–	–	0.4
Medical and public service delivery	7.1	9.1	8.5
Government	*4.5*	*5.7*	*9.0*
Flood studies	–	–	0.1
Physical resource evaluation	3.6	3.9	5.5
Intergovernmental programs	0.9	1.8	3.4
Technological Diffusion	*18.4*	*28.5*	*37.3*
Technology utilization program	7.5	16.0	19.5
National Technical Information Service	10.9	12.5	17.8

SOURCE: *Annual Report to the President and Congress,* 1976. National Center for Productivity and Quality of Working Life, pp. 72–73.

Table 10.2. Total Investment in the U.S. Economy, by Major Type and Source of Finance
(in billions of dollars and percentages of GNP)

	1929		1948		1969	
	$ billions	Percentage of GNP	$ billions	Percentage of GNP	$ billions	Percentage of GNP
Total Investment	45.9	36.1	123.5	37.7	554.0	44.4
Privately financed	40.0	31.4	106.0	32.4	413.6	33.1
Government-financed	5.9	4.6	17.5	5.3	140.4	11.3
Tangible investment[b]	30.2	23.7	78.5	24.0	286.3	22.9
(government-financed)	2.9	2.3	8.2	2.5	54.9	4.4
Intangible investment	15.7	12.3	45.0	13.7	267.8	21.5
(government-financed)	3.0	2.3	9.2	2.8	85.5	6.9
Research and development	0.25	0.2	2.4	0.7	26.2	2.1
(government-financed)	0.07	0.1	1.3	0.4	15.1	1.2
Education and training	11.0	8.6	30.8	9.4	192.4	15.4
(government–financed)	2.5	2.0	6.6	2.0	62.4	5.0
Health and mobility[c]	4.4	3.5	11.8	3.6	49.2	3.9
(government-financed)	0.4	0.3	1.4	0.5	8.0	0.7
Gross National Product, Adjusted[a]	127.3	100.0	327.7	100.0	1,247.9	100.0

NOTE: Detail may not add to totals because of rounding.

a. The official GNP estimates have been adjusted upward to include certain types of investment and imputed rental values of nonbusiness capital goods not included in the Commerce Department estimates.

b. Includes expenditures for new construction, durable goods, and inventory accumulation—by households and governments, as well as by business enterprises.

c. Includes only half of total medical and health expenditures as investment.

SOURCE: John W. Kendrick, *The Formation and Stocks of Total Capital*, pp. 76, 86–87.

If this is so, then policy to promote productivity also means policies to promote continuing increases in investment. To the extent that the investments are privately financed, government encourages investment by maintaining an environment favorable to the private enterprise system. But as table 10.2 shows, a large and rising fraction of intangible investment has been publicly financed. Thus government can, through its own expenditures, directly produce the rising trend of investments required for productivity advance. Public investments may be justified when the benefits would not accrue primarily to the firms that might undertake them but rather to the broader community, or when the outlays take a long time to pay off and involve higher risk than private enterprises are ordinarily willing to bear.

The growing role of public investment places an obligation on government not to engage in "stop and go" financing, such as the cutback in public R&D outlays in the latter 1960s that increased the unemployment of scientists and engineers. Rather, public policy should be directed toward a steady increase in the required investments that have a significant payoff but are not undertaken by the private sectors. An R&D tax credit to stimulate private R&D outlays has also been proposed. It is to be hoped that the Science Adviser to the President and the Office of Science and Technology Policy, which was reestablished in the fall of 1976 after a lapse of several years, will develop effective policy recommendations in this area.

Note that tangible investments have remained a fairly constant proportion of GNP in good years. Actually, tangible investment would tend to decline if research and development were not undertaken to develop profitable investment opportunities in new and better products and processes. Maintenance of a high level of tangible investment is desirable because new plants and equipment are the carriers of new technology. In recent years the federal government has encouraged tangible investment by granting investment tax credits and accelerated depreciation allowances, by which the profitability of new investment is enhanced.

Other Routes to Higher Productivity

Not all productivity advance entails investment expenditures. Of the several other sources of increase, economies of scale may

115

be mentioned first. Such economies accompany growth as increasing specialization of workers, machines, plants, and firms occurs and as certain types of overhead functions need not expand in proportion to output. However, since the optimum rate of growth is determined by other factors, particularly the saving and investment propensities of the community, it is not reasonable to try to accelerate productivity by accelerating growth above the optimum rate. Yet the growth rate will be somewhat higher if it is relatively steady and is not unduly interrupted by cyclical recessions, as noted above. Thus, policies to achieve a steadier, higher growth rate are indicated because they will produce greater economies of scale and larger cumulative investment.

It must be noted, however, that the effect of scale economies accompanying growth would be partly offset by a decline in the average quality of land and other natural resources used in production. In principle, productivity is also affected by the average inherent quality of human resources (apart from human investments); but presumably the average potential of human beings does not change much over the centuries, although changes in the age composition of the labor force may have a short-term impact.

Finally, by increasing economic efficiency, the nation also increases productivity. This objective is achieved by improving the allocation of resources relative to an optimum allocation. As far as resources used in current production are concerned, this means improving competition in the enterprise sector and removing restrictions on mobility of resources, as discussed above. In the regulated sector, it means improving regulatory procedures and rules in order better to simulate the results of competition. In the government and the private nonprofit sectors, it means better cost-benefit analysis, so that the disposition of public funds will better conform to the community's perferences.

Perhaps even more important from the viewpoint of long-run growth and productivity improvement is the efficient allocation of resources released by saving among the various types of investment and among the various sectors and industries performing the investment activities—in order to increase future production and productivity. With regard to types of investment this is not easy to do, particularly for the intangible investments in education and health that are undertaken for nonpecuniary reasons as well as to enhance income-producing potential. Ideally, to the extent calculations are possible, investments of each type should be carried to the point where they promise to yield the same rate of return, which should equal or exceed the interest rate on borrowing or the cost of other sources of funds.

The same rule applies to the allocation of investment funds among sectors or industries. But application of the rule is complicated by the differing structures of industries. Many of the service industries, for example, consist of large numbers of small enterprises that are not big enough to be able to conduct significant amounts of research and development or to make other kinds of intangible investment. As a result, very little such investment is undertaken and, as we saw in chapter 5, rates of productivity advance in such service industries are well below the national average. It has been proposed that these firms could conduct joint R & D through their trade associations (consistent with antitrust laws), possibly with matching funds from the federal government. Certainly agriculture, which also consists of many relatively small components, has been greatly aided by federal programs, including research and extension services.

Small businesses also have often experienced difficulties in obtaining loans to finance tangible investments in inventories, plants, and equipment. Since the 1930s various federal credit agencies have been created to make direct loans or to guarantee loans made by private financial institutions; by fiscal year 1972 these agencies were involved in loans totaling many billions of dollars. In addition there is the Small Business Administration, which was set up to help small nonfarm businesses with their problems, just as the Department of Agriculture seeks to assist farmers to operate more efficiently. These programs, which facilitate the mobility of capital, can be justified if the benefits exceed the subsidy.

Finally, it appears that governments at all levels are not investing enough in the ways and means required to improve their own productivity. Better procedures are needed to appraise the potential cost-savings that could be achieved from new invest-ments—for purposes of budgeting the capital outlays and then for charging the capital costs to current government accounts. With governments now employing about one-sixth of the work-ers of the nation, it is time that systematic attention be paid to increasing the productivity of government agencies. First steps in this direction are discussed in the next chapter.

Mitigating the Unfavorable Impacts of Technological Progress

The technological and organizational innovations that underlie productivity advance have various undesirable side effects on the economy and society, and these must be dealt with. In the first place there are undesirable effects on the natural environ-ment that are due in part to productivity advance; certain technologies, as well as the increasing physical volume of production, may aggravate pollution problems and increase the draft on irreplaceable natural resources. Second, as pointed out in chapter 5, technology is the most important dynamic element in the economy; it produces continual shifts in demand and supply conditions and thus in the occupational, industrial, and geographical structure of the economy, with consequent im-pacts on human resources. Finally, continual economic changes and the concomitant developments, such as the growth of metropolitan areas, produce problems in the social environment. These are very large problems, and we can do no more here than to mention briefly some of the major recent initiatives that have been undertaken to help ameliorate their impacts.

Concern with the environment goes back many decades, but the environmental movement of the 1960s resulted in the pass-age of laws by many states and the federal government setting standards and restricting polluting practices. The capstone of federal efforts was the establishment in December 1970 of the U.S. Environmental Protection Agency (EPA). Through its ten regional offices, the EPA establishes and enforces environ-mental standards and administers programs relating to air and water pollution, solid wastes management, pesticides, radiation, and noise.

118

The EPA also conducts and sponsors research on pollution and pollution control, and it monitors and analyzes the environment. In addition, the EPA provides technical and financial assistance to state, regional, and local jurisdictions. It provides training, in its own facilities and through outside educational institutions, to develop the skilled manpower required for both public and industry environmental programs. Besides the EPA, there is the Council on Environmental Quality, which advises the president on policy matters.[1]

In 1970, some $9.3 billion was spent on pollution abatement, two-thirds of it from public funds.[2] By 1975 expenditures had risen to more than $18 billion, or about 1.5 percent of GNP. Eventually, outlays to offset pollution and improve the natural environment may rise to 3 percent of the GNP. But this is no more than the increment to GNP produced by one good year's productivity increase. It is clear that the United States can afford the costs, through either taxes or higher prices. The important thing is that standards be set realistically so that the benefits exceed the costs.

Government involvement with facilitating manpower adjustments to economic change goes back a long way. A major landmark was the establishment of the U.S. Employment Service in 1933 to provide a nationwide system of federal-state placement services. The Social Security Act of 1935, providing for a contributory federal-state unemployment insurance system, was of importance in helping the transitionally unemployed as well as those unemployed for cyclical reasons. The counter-cyclical payments pattern was also valuable as a built-in economic stabilizer. Another major push in manpower programs came with the Manpower Development and Training Act of 1962 and subsequent legislation. In the decade from 1962 to 1972, federal outlays for manpower programs expanded almost twentyfold.[3]

The counseling, retraining, and placement services of the federal government were consolidated under the Comprehensive Employment and Training Act (CETA) in 1973. These activities are now administered by states and local areas; the federal government provides funds, general supervision, and auditing of expenditures. Training may be either classroom instruction or on-the-job training. In some geographic areas, moving expenses are provided. CETA programs are heavily oriented toward the poor and disadvantaged. The U.S. Employment Service also provides testing and counseling of applicants as well as placement services.

A complementary approach to human problems in depressed areas was provided by the Public Works and Economic Development Act of 1965. This act authorized funds in the Department of Commerce for the Economic Development Agency (EDA), which coordinates and directs federal activities for stimulating area redevelopment so that new growth industries may replace the older declining industries in providing employment for the residents of depressed areas.

Finally, the Trade Act of 1974 provides adjustment assistance to workers (or unions), firms (or industries), and communities affected by increased imports. Under this act, the EDA administers loans and guarantees to trade-impacted firms and grants to communities that are significantly affected. The Office of Trade Adjustment in the Department of Labor administers adjustment assistance to workers—training grants, job search assistance, and relocation assistance. Adjustment grants under this act are more generous than provided under earlier legislation.

Even this cursory and selective review indicates that governments have gradually come to accept responsibility for bearing a significant portion of the costs of labor adjustments associated with job displacement that results from technological and other dynamic change. Given the major increments to income contributed by productivity growth, it is only fair that most of the attendant costs should be borne by society rather than by the individuals who are affected, generally through no fault of their own.

11

Organizational Policies
to Promote and Accommodate Productivity Advance

The individual producing organization is where the action is with regard to improving operating efficiency under given technologies and making the cost-reducing innovations required for continuing productivity advance. The social mileu in general, and the legal and institutional framework provided by governments in particular, condition the operations of enterprises and other organizations. But given the social and governmental backdrop, it is the degree of efficiency and innovativeness with which producing organizations are managed that largely determines the rate of productivity advance in any economy.

In recent years, increasing numbers of firms have instituted productivity measurement and improvement programs designed to supplement and enhance management's continuing efforts to reduce costs and to increase productivity and thus competitiveness. Although the following discussion centers on company programs, we shall also refer to internal government programs (which would have relevance to private nonprofit institutions as well). We do not enter the domain of household productivity. But it is worth noting that the efficiency with which household members make purchases, invest in appliances and other laborsaving devices, and combine the capital services and intermediate products with their own labor services (and possibly hired labor) in order to create consumption utilities has a direct bearing on ultimate levels of economic welfare.

Since productivity improvement programs are often linked with efforts to measure organizational productivity, we shall start with that topic.

Measuring Organizational Productivity

To a major extent, the data required to produce productivity estimates are available from the records ordinarily maintained by firms and other organizations. Thus, productivity measurement may be developed as part of broader management information systems. The productivity estimates provide another management tool that has a number of important uses.

Like other parts of an information system, the productivity data become part of a feedback loop. By furnishing information on an important aspect of organizational performance—changes in the efficiency with which inputs (or cost elements) are used in the production process—they can signal the need for corrective action if they fall below targeted goals, or norms. They also provide the means for measuring the effects of initiatives taken to improve productivity performance. If the productivity ratios are prepared with respect to a detailed set of inputs, they can pinpoint the areas in which little or no progress is being made in reducing real costs per unit of output. Similarly, if they are prepared for the various divisions, plants, and cost-centers of a firm, they indicate the relative performance of the various organizational units.

It should be stressed that the productivity data do not supplant but merely supplement other efficiency measures. They are, for example, quite distinct from "work measurement," by which actual performance of work groups or individuals is charted against statistical or engineering norms, under given technologies. When equipment or any other aspect of technology changes, the norms are changed accordingly. In contrast, the productivity measures show the improvements in output-input relations resulting from improvements in technological and organizational efficiency, as well as the changes in efficiency under given technologies. Thus, the productivity ratios can be used to establish targets, or "bogeys," that take account of potential technological innovations as well as of improvements in performance under given technological conditions. The company and establishment productivity measures also make possible comparisons with productivity changes in the industry or industries within which the company operates.

Summaries of the firm's productivity results should be disseminated at least within management circles. Perhaps the chief benefit of a productivity measurement system is its psychological effect—increasing the productivity-consciousness of the employees, particularly the management and supervisory personnel. If the measurement system is linked to company-wide productivity improvement programs, discussed in the next section, benefit can be derived by channeling increased productivity-mindedness into efficiency-promoting efforts throughout the work force. To maximize the effectiveness of the measures, summaries should be prepared at least quarterly, and possibly monthly—although seasonal and erratic elements may obscure the underlying trends in monthly estimates. Even annual estimates are useful.

The desirability of productivity measurement is particularly great in governmental and private nonprofit organizations; such organizations do not generate profit measures, which are the ultimate indicator of performance in the enterprise sector. But even in business firms, levels of and changes in productivity are a major element influencing the actual levels or changes in profit rates of a firm relative to its competition, since they all sell and buy at much the same prices. So the productivity measures may provide early warnings of problems that could impact unfavorably on profits.

For example, the executive vice president of Mill Products of the Aluminum Company of America wrote in a paper referring to the measurement system his division installed in 1968,

> It was a terrible shock to discover that although output per man-hour in Alcoa has increased 20% from 1958 to 1965, the increase in the industry for the same time period was about 60%. Believe me, that stimulated real action on our part. . . . The record since 1968 would indicate that the mechanism used in Mill Products

to insure productivity growth has been relatively effective . . . measured against our 1968 base, output per man-hour in Alcoa's Mill Products has increased more than the output per man-hour of the aluminum rolling and drawing industry as a whole. If that were not the case, I might not be here to tell you about it.[1]

Another use of productivity measures is as a background for budgeting and long-range projections. Based on past trends, modified by the anticipated effects of planned organizational and technological innovations, productivity projections—in conjunction with sales and output projections—enable future requirements for labor and other inputs to be estimated. Such projections are useful in planning personnel recruitment, training, investment, and procurement programs. Then, when the future input estimates are multiplied by projected wage-rates and other input prices, cost estimates are obtained for budgeting purposes.

Although company productivity measurement has spread in the past decade, there still are many companies that have not availed themselves of it. This is due in part to lack of knowledge of the required measurement techniques. There are several manuals, listed in the bibliography, that explain methodology. At least one gives illustrative case studies.[2] The U.S. Department of Commerce has sponsored lectures on the subject in major cities, and there are a number of consulting firms and individuals who assist firms in designing their measurement systems. In the federal government, the Bureau of Labor Statistics has taken over measurement of agency productivity. The National Center for Productivity and Quality of Working Life seeks to encourage state and local governments to measure their productivity and has published reports on productivity in various areas of governmental function.

It is not intended to provide specific measurement instructions in this book—nor is it necessary in view of the available manuals, including one coauthored by the present writer (see note 2)—but a few general comments are in order. With respect to measuring output of enterprises, either of two equivalent approaches may be adopted. Data on the physical volume of outputs in each product category may be combined, weighted by relative prices as of a given base period. Or the value of production (sales or shipments plus the value of the change in inventories of finished and in-process goods) may be "deflated" by an index of the prices of the products. The base period chosen for the quantity weights or the price index number usually is a recent, relatively normal year or an average for several years. In the case of general governments, however, since goods and services are not sold in markets, the price deflation approach is not feasible. Nor are prices available for weighting. Rather, numbers of units of the various categories of services may be weighted by costs per unit of each in the base period.

Rather than subtract the real cost of purchased materials, supplies, and outside services from the real value of gross output in order to obtain real value added (net output), it is better to relate *gross* output to all inputs. The total productivity measures are preferable from the viewpoint of enterprise managers, since they are trying to conserve in all cost elements —intermediate products as well as factor services. Further, substitutions are made among all inputs in response to changes in relative prices as well as in technology.

The real volume of intermediate product inputs is measured in the same way as outputs—since these inputs are the outputs of others. The inputs of the labor factor are usually measured in terms of hours worked, not hours paid for, since increasing the number of hours paid for but not worked is an indirect way of increasing compensation per hour worked, which is what managements are paying for. Capital inputs are usually assumed to move proportionately to the real stocks of structures, equipment, inventories, and land used in production. The inputs are combined on the basis of their proportions of total costs, including normal profits or, in the case of government and nonprofit organizations, an imputed interest charge on total assets. Index numbers of output are then divided by index numbers of total input and of each input class, in order to obtain the total and partial productivity ratios.

Productivity Improvement Programs

For more than fifty years, various U.S. companies have instituted and operated special programs designed to improve productivity, in an attempt to involve many or all employees in the continuing drive to reduce costs. The programs have been based on the simple premise that labor-management cooperation in promoting efficiency is vital to the success of the enterprise and that it is to the benefit both of owners and management in securing adequate returns on investment and of labor in providing job security and competitive wages and working conditions. "It is believed that such cooperation, if successful, taps a deep reservoir of knowledge and experience among the underlying work force that is not ordinarily available to management. It is thought also that successful labor-management cooperation arrangements serve to stimulate worker efficiency in the performance of day-to-day job duties."[3]

The development of productivity programs was facilitated by the maturing of industrial unionism to a stage at which cooperation with management to improve production techniques, increase efficiency, and reduce waste could accompany defensive and bargaining activities. Programs were initiated in nonunion plants and firms as well. But most of the early examples of joint labor-management committees before World War II were found in unionized firms that were experiencing financial difficulties. A major impetus to the movement came with World War II; in March 1942 the chairman of the War Production Board (WPB) urged the creation of "joint management-labor committees to push production up to and beyond the President's goals."[4] The idea was endorsed by major union and employee organizations. In total, about 5,000 committees in plants employing over 7 million workers registered with the WPB. But only about 1,000 committees directly addressed productivity problems. Other activities included the more efficient use of raw materials and the reworking, recovery, or salvage of materials; design of tools and of products; improvements in the maintenance, repair, and use of equipment; technological innovations; adjustments to changes in work assignments; handling problems of safety and absenteeism. Appraisals of the results of the joint committees' activities were generally favorable.[5] Nevertheless, in 1948 a survey conducted by the BLS indicated that only about one-third of the wartime committees were still operating, about 20 percent of them in nonunion plants. Apparently there were more discontinuances in subsequent years. Beginning in the 1950s, there was a gradual increase in the number of plants operating under a new form of labor-management cooperation called the Scanlon Plan. Also using a committee structure to obtain worker participation in cost reduction, the plan involved a system of plant-wide bonus payments based on estimated savings in labor costs. After twenty years, about 500 plants in the United States and Canada are using plans of this type. Another major impetus to the use of productivity committees came in 1971 when, faced with increasing foreign competition, the major basic steel companies and the United Steelworkers of America agreed to establish a joint advisory committee on employment security and plant productivity at each plant of the signatory companies. The provision was carried over into the three-year collective bargaining contract reached in May 1974, which states, "The future for the industry in terms of employment security and return on substantial capital expenditures will rest heavily upon the ability of the parties to work cooperatively to achieve significantly higher productivity trends than have occurred in the recent past." The functions of the committees, which meet monthly, "shall be to advise with plant management concerning ways and means of improving productivity and developing recommendations for stimulating its growth so as to promote the purposes of the parties as set forth above and also promote orderly and peaceful relations with the employees, to achieve uninterrupted operations in the plants, to promote the use of domestic steel and to achieve the desired prosperity and progress of the Company and its employees."[6] It is specified that the functioning of the committees shall not affect the rights of either party under other provisions of the agreement.

Other unions have concluded similar agreements. A BLS survey showed that as of mid-1973 there were sixty-four agreements covering more than 500,000 workers providing for joint productivity committees; this does not include plans of the Scanlon type, small agreements (covering fewer than 1,000 workers), productivity programs in nonunion firms, or govern-

127

mental programs. Nevertheless, it can not be claimed that joint productivity committees are widely used to promote efficiency in industry or government.

Since there is a great potential for cooperative productivity programs, in what follows we shall summarize some of the main characteristics of existing programs. The description is based largely on a series of case studies published by the National Center. [7]

The productivity improvement programs, most of which involve joint labor-management committees or teams, often were initiated in response to serious problems facing a firm. We have mentioned the increasing severity of foreign competition in the steel industry; United States Steel is one of the National Cennter's case studies. Another example is the Beech Aircraft Corporation, which formalized its program in 1964 in response to an appeal of President Lyndon B. Johnson, who called on all defense contractors to establish an affirmative program of cost reduction in performance of defense contracts. Detroit Edison established its ACTION (All Committed to Improving Operations Now) program in 1972 under pressure of rising costs and of the Michigan Public Service Commission, which grants rate increases conditional on a company's active pursuit of efforts to improve operating efficiency. Honeywell, Inc., initiated its Productivity Improvement Program in 1973 as a "partial but an important" answer to "unbelievable world-wide inflation" and in an effort to strengthen its competitive position and provide greater flexibility in response to changing economic conditions.[8] The Thiem Corporation's programs grew out of the personal philosophy and experience of its executives.

The programs were initiated by the chief executives with participation by top management and, in the case of joint committees, by union leaders. It was considered important to do considerable advance planning for the organization, operation, and monitoring of programs. Occasionally, outside consultants were brought in. Training courses were conducted in some instances for middle management and supervisors in productivity concepts, measurement, and promotional methods. At Honeywell, two-day seminars or a series of two- to three-hour workshops were used. The training materials formed the basis of a productivity manual issued early in 1975.

At the heart of the programs is involvement of personnel at all levels, through joint committees or teams in plants, departments, and offices. It is through the committees that problems are discussed and suggestions received and screened. The committees provide the contact points with the employees, who are kept informed of activities and results through bulletins, newsletters, films, and meetings. The committees and/or organizational units set up by management may set goals and periodically review and evaluate results of the program as revealed by measures of productivity and related variables. Measurement techniques may be expanded in scope and coverage as part of the program. For example, by October 1974 some 80 percent of Detroit Edison's employees were covered by work measures, compared with 50 percent eighteen moths earlier at the inception of ACTION. It must be recognized, however, that some functions are not amenable to measurement.

The areas on which productivity improvement programs focus are primarily those in which worker involvement may result in improved labor efficiency or in an increased flow of innovative ideas. A particularly fruitful area is that of work simplification, based on the premise that no one knows a job as well as the person doing it. Beech Aircraft, for example, found that after employees had been given some training in the basic tools and techniques used by industrial engineers, there was no stopping them. Suggestions made to eliminate unnecessary operations and to use better and simpler methods in plant and office may mean small savings on an individual basis but substantial savings in total. Ideas for job redesign and enrichment may be solicited, too.

Workers are also a source of ideas for improving the design of machinery and equipment, reducing machine set-up time, downtime, and maintenance cost. The cooperation of the work force is likewise important in conservation and waste-reduction programs, salvage activity, and achieving "zero defects" goals. Joint committee activities help in reducing accidents, absenteeism, and tardiness. Where feasible, use of flexi-time schedules and part-time workers promotes the same ends. Labor cooperation is also essential to expanding work measurement and development of standards. Worker participation is helpful in planning training programs.

Although the Scanlon Plan and certain profit-sharing plans provide plant-wide or company-wide bonuses based on a portion of the cost-savings or profits that accrue from increased productivity, most programs provide cash awards to individuals or work groups for specific successful cost-reduction suggestions. In all programs, stress is placed on providing due recognition to individuals and groups for superior ideas and performance. [9]

In addition to having direct impacts on productivity, the joint labor-management committees were found to be of considerable value as channels of communication. They often served as a means of resolving minor problems before they mushroomed into major labor relations issues. Good communication between the committees and the rank-and-file workers was essential to eliciting broad participation in the activities.

It should be emphasized that broad-based productivity improvement programs merely supplement usual management efforts to develop and implement innovations that center on the selection and planning of R&D and capital expenditure programs. The joint committee activities are essentially advisory. But they have proved their value in many cases and serve to enhance management's own productivity-consciousness.

Joint productivity committees have also operated in selected federal agencies and in state and municipal governments. In the federal government in July 1973, the Office of Management and Budget established a continuing productivity program, the Joint Financial Management Improvement Program (JFMIP), which was authorized to prepare annual reports analyzing the reasons for the productivity changes revealed by the measurement program described earlier and to prepare recommendations and plans for future productivity improvements. For example, in its 1975 annual report, JFMIP outlined plans for an interchange of ideas on productivity improvement opportunities, through on-site visits with private firms in selected industries that have functions in common with government. Workshops were also planned with state and local government officials in such areas as general services, real property maintenance, and vehicle maintenance.

Experience has shown that after an initial period of fruitful operation while the reservoir of preexisting ideas is being tapped, productivity improvement programs tend to slow down. At this point, it is important to maintain the organizational apparatus in order to encourage and facilitate a continuing flow of innovative ideas and actions, even though committee meetings may be required less frequently than in the early stages.

Perhaps the chief obstacle to successful implementation of productivity improvement plans is the fear of workers that more productive work may reduce employment and thus threaten their job security. Such fears have been reflected in restrictive work rules negotiated by some unions and in restrictive work practices by nonunion as well as union workers in some industries. They have also been reflected in an increasing tendency of unions to seek a voice in management's planning of the introduction of labor-saving machinery.

This points up the desirability of assurances—and guarantees where feasible—by management that productivity-enhancing programs will not result in layoffs. Actually, as noted in chapter 5, industries with above-average productivity increases have tended to increase employment more than those with below-average productivity. The same is true of firms; labor has more to fear from technologically backward managements than from progressive ones. Usually, the technological displacement of particular jobs can be accommodated within firms by retraining and reassigning workers.[10] Even when total employment of a company declines moderately, normal turnover can make layoffs unnecessary. Procedures in these respects have been increasingly formalized in collective bargaining agreements. So also have provisions for severance pay when layoffs cannot be avoided. In addition, companies often provide counseling for departing employees and call attention to the various government programs that are available to them (as discussed in chapter 10) and possible job opportunities in other organizations.

Notes

Chapter 2

1. Edward F. Denison, *Accounting for United States Economic Growth, 1929–1929* (Washington: Brookings Institution, 1974), p. 111.
2. See "The Measurement of Productivity," *Survey of Current Business* Pt. II (May 1972). This also includes comments by Denison on the work of Jorgenson and Griliches and replies by them.

Chapter 3

1. Adam Smith, *The Wealth of Nations* (New York: Random House, 1937), p. 326.
2. Carrol D. Wright, *Industrial Depressions*, First Annual Report of the Commissioner of Labor, Bureau of Labor, U.S. Department of Interior (Washington: Government Printing Office, 1886), p. 80.
3. The first of the studies was Frederick C. Mills, *Economic Tendencies in the United States* (New York: National Bureau of Economic Research, 1932). The summary study, which built on and refers to the many industry studies sponsored by the bureau, was John W. Kendrick, *Productivity Trends in the United States* (Princeton: Princeton University Press, for the National Bureau of Economic Research, 1961).
4. See National Research Project, Works Progress Administration, *Production, Employment, and Productivity in 59 Manufacturing Industries, 1919–36*, Report No. S-1 (Philadelphia: Works Progress Administration, May 1939).
5. See John A. Gorman, "Non-financial Corporations: New Measures of Output and Input," *Survey of Current Business*, March 1972.
6. See B. Vaccara and J. Kendrick, eds., *New Developments in Productivity Measurement*, Studies in Income and Wealth series (New York: National Bureau of Economic Research, forthcoming).
7. See *Productivity Centers around the World* (Washington: National Commission on Productivity and Work Quality, May 1975), p. 5. Much of the material in this section has been drawn from this booklet.
8. Ibid., p. iii.
9. See *Third Annual Report*, National Commission on Productivity and Work Quality (Washington: Government Printing Office, March 1974), p. 11.

Chapter 4

1. U.S. productivity growth from 1800 through 1889 is believed to have averaged less than 0.5 percent a year. See M. Abramovitz and Paul A. David, *Economic Growth in America: Historical Parables and Realities* (Stanford, Cal.: Stanford University Center for Research in Economic Growth, 1973).

2. This section is taken from material prepared by the author for the Joint Economic Committee, U.S. Congress, *U.S. Economic Growth from 1976 to 1986: Prospects, Problems, and Patterns*, vol. 1, *Productivity* (Washington: Government Printing Office, October 1976).

3. See Edward F. Denison, *Accounting for United States Economic Growth, 1929–1969* (Washington: Brookings Institution, 1974), tables 8–2 and 8–5. See also table 7.1, ch. 7.

4. See John W. Kendrick, "The Productivity Slowdown," *Business Economics*, September 1971.

5. Frank Gollop and Dale W. Jorgenson. "U.S. Total Factor Productivity by Industry, 1949–1973," in *New Developments in Productivity Measurement*, Studies in Income and Wealth (New York: National Bureau of Economic Research, forthcoming).

6. "Economic Growth and Total Capital Formation," a study prepared for the Subcommittee on Economic Growth of the Joint Economic Committee, U.S. Congress (Washington: Government Printing Office, February 1976).

Chapter 5

1. See Bureau of the Budget, Office of the President, *Measuring Productivity of Federal Government Organizations* (Washington: Government Printing Office, 1964).

2. See John W. Kendrick, *Productivity Trends in the United States* (Princeton: Princeton University Press), pp. 177–87; and *Postwar Productivity Trends in the United States, 1948–1969* (New York: National Bureau of Economic Research, 1973), pp. 132–43.

Chapter 6

1. See Edward F. Denison, assisted by Jean-Pierre Poullier, *Why Growth Rates Differ* (Washington: Brookings Institution, 1967).

Chapter 7

1. See Frank Gollop and Dale W. Jorgenson, "U.S. Total Factor Productivity by Industry, 1947–1973," in *New Developments in Productivity Measurement*, Studies in Income and Wealth (New York: National Bureau of Economic Research, forthcoming); and L. Christensen, D. Cummings, and D. Jorgenson, "An International Comparison of Growth in Productivity, 1947–1973," papers prepared for the Conference on New Developments in Productivity Measurement, Williamsburg, November 1975 (New York: National Bureau of Economic Research, mimeograph).

2. See John W. Kendrick, *The Formation and Stocks of Total Capital* (New York: National Bureau of Economic Research, 1976); see also table 10.2, ch. 10.

3. Edward F. Denison, *Accounting for United States Economic Growth, 1929–1969* (Washington: Brookings Institution, 1974).

Chapter 8

1. These and the subsequent numbers come from John W. Kendrick, *Postwar Productivity Trends in the United States, 1948–1969* (New York: National Bureau of Economic Research, 1973).

2. Wesley C. Mitchell, *Business Cycles* (Berkeley: University of California Press, 1913).

3. See Geoffrey H. Moore, "Productivity, Costs, and Prices: New Light for an Old Hypothesis," *Explorations in Economic Research* II, no. 1 (Winter 1975).

4. See Bureau of Economic Analysis, U.S. Department of Commerce, *Business Conditions Digest*, November 1976, p. 100.

Chapter 9

1. Much of this section is drawn from material prepared by the author for the Joint Economic Committee, U.S. Congress, "Productivity Trends and Prospects," in *U.S. Economic Growth from 1976 to 1986: Prospects, Problems, and Patterns*, vol. 1, *Productivity* (Washington: Government Printing Office, October 1976).

2. See J. Meyers, L. Nakamura, and N. Madrid, "The Impact of OPEC, EPA, and OSHA on Productivity and Growth," *Conference Board Record* vol. XIII, no. 4, April 1976.

3. *The Future of Productivity*, proceedings of a symposium sponsored by the National Center for Productivity and Quality of Working Life (Washington, 1977).

4. Bureau of Labor Statistics, U.S. Department of Labor, "The Structure of the U.S. Economy in 1980 and 1985," Bulletin 1831 (Washington: Government Printing Office, 1975).

Chapter 10

1. A good summary description of EPA activities is contained in its pamphlet, *Toward a New Environmental Ethic* (Washington: Government Printing Office, 1972).

2. See *Improving the Quality of Life: A Study of the Economics of Pollution Control* (Chase Manhattan Bank, 1972; free on request from the Public Relations Division of the bank, One Chase Manhattan Plaza, New York, N.Y. 10015.

3. See Sar Levitan, G. Mangum, and R. Marshall, *Human Resources and Labor Markets* (New York: Harper and Row, 1973), table 16–1, pp. 320–21.

Chapter 11

1. As quoted in *Improving Productivity through Industry and Company Measurement* (Washington: National Center for Productivity and Quality of Working Life, October 1976), p. 40.

2. See John W. Kendrick and Daniel Creamer, *Measuring Company Productivity: Handbook with Case Studies* (New York: Conference Board, 1965).

3. *Labor-Management Productivity Committees in American Industry* (Washington: National Commission on Productivity and Work Quality, May 1975), p. 2.

4. See Dorothea de Schweinitz, *Labor and Management in a Common Enterprise* (Cambridge: Harvard University Press, 1949), cited in ibid, p. 11.

5. *Labor-Management Productivity Committees in American Industry*, pp. 11–13.

6. Ibid., pp. 31–2.

7. *Improving Productivity: A Description of Selected Company Programs*, Series 1 (Washington: National Center for Productivity and Quality of Working Life, December 1975).

8. Ibid., p. 15.

9. The argument that monetary incentives must be central to efforts to improve productivity is developed by Mitchell Fein, *Rational Approaches to Raising Productivity* (Norcross, Georgia: American Institute of Industrial Engineers, 1974).

10. See Bureau of Labor Statistics, U.S. Department of Labor, *Studies of Automatic Technology* (Washington: Government Printing Office, 1966).

Bibliography

General

Abramovitz, Moses. "Resource and Output Trends in the United States since 1870." Occasional Paper no. 52. New York: National Bureau of Economic Research, 1956.

Brown, Murray. *On the Theory and Measurement of Technological Change.* Cambridge: At the University Press, 1965.

———, ed. *The Theory and Empirical Analysis of Production*, Studies in Income and Wealth, vol. 31. New York: National Bureau of Economic Research, 1967.

Conference on Research in Income and Wealth. *Output, Input, and Productivity Measurement.* Studies in Income and Wealth, vol. 25. Princeton University Press, for National Bureau of Economic Research, 1961.

Davis, Hiram S. *Productivity Accounting.* Philadelphia: University of Pennsylvania Press, 1956.

Denison, Edward F. *Accounting for United States States Economic Growth, 1929–1969.* Washington: Brookings Institution, 1974.

———. "Some Major Issues in Productivity Analysis: An Examination of Estimates by Jorgenson and Griliches." *Survey of Current Business*, pt. II, May 1969.

———. *The Source of Economic Growth in the United States and the Alternatives before Us.* Supplementary Paper no. 13. New York: Committee for Economic Development, 1962.

———. *Why Growth Rates Differ.* Washington: Brookings Institution, 1967.

Duerinck, G. *Productivity Measurement*, vol. I, *Concepts.* Project no. 235. Paris: European Productivity Agency, 1955.

Dunlop, John T., ed. *Automation and Technological Change.* Englewood Cliffs, N.J.: Prentice Hall, for American Assembly, 1962.

Dunlop, John T., and Diatchenko, V. P., eds. *Labor Productivity.* New York: McGraw-Hill, 1964.

Fabricant, S. *Primer on Productivity.* New York: Random House, 1971.

Frankel, M. *British and American Productivity: A Comparison and Interpretation.* Urbana: University of Illinois Press, 1957.

Fuchs, Victor R. *The Service Economy.* New York: National Bureau of Economic Research, 1968.

136

———, ed. *Production and Productivity in the Service Industries.* New York: Columbia University Press, 1965.

Gold, Bela. *Foundations of Productivity Analysis.* Pittsburgh: University of Pittsburgh Press, 1955.

Gorman, John A. "Non-financial Corporations: New Measures of Output and Input." *Survey of Current Business,* March 1972.

Hagedorn, George G. *Productivity: Gauge of Economic Performance.* New York: National Association of Manufacturers, 1955.

Hollander, S. *The Sources of Increased Efficiency.* Boston: M.I.T. Press, 1965.

Hultgren, Thor. *Costs, Prices, and Profits: Their Cyclical Relations.* New York: National Bureau of Economic Research, 1965.

Hutton, D. G. *We Too Can Prosper: The Promise of Productivity.* London: George Allen and Unwin, 1953.

Kendrick, John W. *Economic Accounts and Their Uses.* New York: McGraw-Hill, 1972.

———. *The Formation and Stocks of Total Capital.* New York: National Bureau of Economic Research, 1976.

———. *Postwar Productivity Trends in the United States, 1948–1969.* New York: National Bureau of Economic Research, 1973.

———. *Productivity Trends in the United States.* Princeton: Princeton University Press, for National Bureau of Economic Research, 1961.

Kendrick, John W., and Creamer, D. *Measuring Company Productivity: Handbook with Case Studies.* Studies in Business Economics no. 89. New York: Conference Board, 1965.

Lave, L. *Technological Change: Its Conception and Measurement.* New York: Prentice-Hall, 1966.

Machlup, Fritz. *The Production and Distribution of Knowledge.* Princeton: Princeton University Press, 1962.

Maddison, Angus. *Economic Growth in the West: Comparative Experience in Europe and North America.* New York: Twentieth Century Fund, 1964.

Mansfield, Edwin. *The Economics of Technological Change.* New York: W. W. Norton, 1968.

Myers, Charles A., ed. *Wages, Prices, Profits, and Productivity.* New York: American Assembly, Columbia University Press, June 1959.

Nadiri, M. I. "Some Approaches to the Theory and Measurement of Total Factor Productivity: A Survey," *Journal of Economic Literature* VIII, no. 4 (December 1970).

Nelson, R.; Peck, M.; and Kalacheck, E. *Technology, Economic Growth, and Public Policy.* Washington: Brookings Institution, 1967.

Rappard, W. E. *The Secret of American Prosperity.* New York: Greenberg Publisher, 1955.

Salter, W. E. G. *Productivity and Technical Change.* Cambridge: At the University Press, 1965; paper, 1969.

Siegel, Irving H. *Concepts and Measurement of Production and Productivity.* Working Paper of the National Conference on Productivity, sponsored by the Bureau of Labor Statistics, U.S. Department of Labor, 1952.

Schmookler, J. *Invention and Economic Growth.* Cambridge: Harvard University Press, 1966.

Terborgh, George. *The Automation Hysteria.* Washington: Machinery and Allied Products Institute and Council for Technological Advancement, 1965.

United States Government
(available from Government Printing Office, Washington, D.C.)

Department of Agriculture. Agriculture Research Service. *Changes in Farm Production and Efficiency.* Annual since 1954.

Department of Commerce. Bureau of Economic Analysis. "The Measurement of Productivity." *Survey of Current Business,* pt. II. May 1972.

Department of Labor. Bureau of Labor Statistics. Indexes of Output per Man-Hour. Selected Industries. Annual since 1958.

——. *Productivity: A Selected. Annotated Bibliography. 1971–75.* Bulletin 1933. 1977. Previous BLS bibliographies on productivity include Bulletin 1226 (1958), Bulletin 1514 (1966), and Bulletin 1776 (1971).

——. *Productivity and Costs.* U.S. Private Business, Farm, Nonfarm, and Manufacturing Sectors. Quarterly since 1966.

——. *Trends in Output per Man-Hour in the Private Economy. 1909–1958.* (Bulletin 2149). 1959, and subsequent annual extensions.

General Accounting Office, with Office of Management and Budget, Civil Service Commission, and Bureau of Labor Statistics. *Measuring and Enhancing Productivity in the Federal Government.* 1973.

Joint Financial Management Improvement Program. *Productivity Programs in the Federal Government.* Annual Report to the President and the Congress. Since 1974.

National Center for Productivity and Quality of Working Life. *Annual Report to the President and Congress.* Since 1976.

——. *Improving Productivity: A Description of Selected Company Programs.* Series 1. December 1975.

National Commission on Productivity and Work Quality. *Annual Report to the President and Congress.* 1971, 1972, 1973, 1974, 1975.

——. *Productivity Centers around the World.* May 1975.

National Commission on Technology, Automation, and Economic Progress. *Report to the President.* 1966.

Office of the President. Bureau of the Budget. *Measuring Productivity of Federal Government Organizations.* 1964.

Index

Library of Congress Cataloging in Publication Data

Kendrick, John W.
   Understanding productivity.

   (Policy studies in employment and welfare ; no. 31)
   Bibliography: p. 136
   Includes index.
   1. Industrial productivity. 2. Industrial productiv-
ity—United States. I. Title.
HD56.K46   338'.0973   77-4786
ISBN 0-8018-1996-2
ISBN 0-8018-1997-0 pbk.